World-Making Stories

World-Making Stories

*Maidu Language and
Community Renewal on a
Shared California Landscape*

EDITED BY M. ELEANOR NEVINS

With contributions from the Weje-ebis
(Keep Speaking) Jamani Maidu Language
Revitalization Project

And Tom Young, Roxie Peconom, Dan Williams,
Maym Gallagher, and Kenneth Holbrook

Adapted from translations by William Shipley

Illustrations by Daniel Stolpe

UNIVERSITY OF NEBRASKA PRESS | LINCOLN AND LONDON

This book is published as part of the Recovering Languages and Literacies of the Americas initiative. Recovering Languages and Literacies is generously supported by the Andrew W. Mellon Foundation.

♾

Library of Congress Control Number: 2017942531

Set in Huronia by Tseng Information Systems, Inc.

This book is dedicated in loving memory to
Farrell Cunningham–jatam (1976–2013), who planted
and grew our work with us at Weje-ebis Maidu.

The vision of my brother's existence was, and is still, brilliant!
Let his light so shine in memory of his life's work.
There is no one who is comparable
to his gifts of knowledge,
to his strength as a leader.
Forever in my heart.

The Weje-ebis Maidu project team requests that
readers of this book respect the expectation among the
Maidu community concerning the names of
the deceased. If speaking Farrell Cunningham's name
aloud, follow with *jatam* (pronounced yah-tam).

"Amám, májdym tét'yt'y kymádom
ka?ámkano,
mínk'i tét'yt'ym, tetébet'yt'ýmyni, uním
k'ódo c'ehéjhejk'ojdom;
japájtodom, amýni,
k'ódo mákpajdom;
amýni, k'ódo jawídom;
adóm, mákpapajtidom tét'yt'y mínk'i
jawímapem," ac'ój?am.

"Myjákkapem k'ódom ka?án,
myjákkapem jamánim ka?án mým'
adóm, ka?ámkano mákpapajtinimmyni,
mí jákk'at mákkitmapem," ac'ój?am.

"Thereupon, being people who have
children,
your children, having gotten a little bigger,
will look about around this country;
speaking well to them, then,
teaching them about the land;
so then, naming the country for them;
just so, you will teach your children to
know names," ac'ój?am.

"This place has a name,
that mountain has a name,
just so, you shall be teaching them,
teaching them to know what you know,"
ac'ój?am.

—**Hánc'ibyjim**, spoken in 1902

CONTENTS

PART ONE. COMMUNITY RENEWAL

PART TWO. CREATION NARRATIVES OF HÁNC'IBYJIM / TOM YOUNG

PART THREE. PRONUNCIATION AND LESSONS

ACKNOWLEDGMENTS

The Weje-ebis project team gratefully acknowledges financial support from the Administration for Native Americans, from the Mellon Foundation's Recovering Languages and Literacies of the Americas, from Middlebury College's Undergraduate Research Office, and from research funds from Middlebury College Dean of Faculty. We also gratefully acknowledge institutional support from Susanville Indian Rancheria in administering the ANA grant, Middlebury College for supporting research and writing, Maidu Intertribal Language Summit (and Donna Clark, who financially supported that effort) for providing a forum for dialogue, and the Maidu Summit Consortium for acting as copyright holder of the work. In addition, we wish to thank Pat Kervick of the archives of the Peabody Ethnological Museum for providing us with copies of Roland Dixon's notebooks, and Jacque Sustrand, the director of the University of Nevada Reno Special Collections, for help accessing and imaging the Shipley and Stolpe volumes. We thank Ilze Akerberg of Indiana University Archives of Traditional Music for providing sound recordings of songs sung for Roland Dixon in 1902 by Tom Young and Bill Reeves, as well as Andrew Garret at the UC Berkeley Survey of California and Other Indian Languages for access to William Shipley's field recordings.

Thanks to the estate of William Shipley for providing us with Bill's unpublished lessons in Maidu and for permission to publish them for the first time here. We also thank the estate of William Shipley for permission to republish his transcriptions, transliterations, and literary translation and for permission to adapt, alter, and re-present these as needed in service of Maidu language learning. We thank Daniel Stolpe for permission to similarly adapt and republish his original artwork for presentation in an affordable paperback. We are grateful to Wilhelmina Ives, elder and Maidu language keeper, for guidance on key issues of translation and place. Thanks to Jim Bauman for advice on language pedagogy and for establishing an online Maidu lexicon from Shipley's text collection and for continuing support via the Maidu site in OurLanguage.org.

We also recognize four undergraduate research assistants at Middlebury College. Thanks to Sophie Bufton and Anna Mullen for recording, interviewing, and photographing accounts of Maidu places with Maidu community members. We also thank Maddie Gilbert, who checked parts 1 and 2 of Shipley's literary transcription and translation against Dixon's text collection and helped restore sentence-by-sentence correspondence and omitted lines. Thanks to Maddie Cochrane, who, with the guidance of project participants, rendered the map at the front of this book that locates key Maidu places with respect to widely recognized landmarks and towns on the shared indigenous-settler landscape. Thanks to Mari Price, Sociology and Anthropology coordinator for typing up Shipley's lessons on reading and pronouncing Maidu for inclusion in this volume. A warm thank you to Matt Bokovoy and Heather Stauffer of the University of Nebraska Press for seeing this project through from beginning to end.

CONTRIBUTORS

1899-1905

Tom Young / Hánc'ibyjim (Genesee CA)

Roland Dixon (Cambridge MA)

Hiriam Kelley (Round Valley CA)

Dorius Leon Spencer (Genesee CA)

Billi Preacher (Chico CA)

George Barber (Chico CA)

Mike Jefferson (Chico CA)

Pouissey (Chico CA)

Mary Azbill (Chico CA)

Henry Azbill (Chico CA)

Bill Reeves (Mooretown CA)

1955-2003

Maym Hannah Gallagher (Paynes Creek CA)

Lena Thomas Benner (Susanville CA)

Roxie Peconom (Susanville CA)

Dan Williams (Quincy CA)

Leone Morales (Susanville CA)

George Peconom (Susanville CA)

Marie Potts (Sacramento CA)

William Shipley (Santa Cruz CA)

Daniel Stolpe (Santa Cruz CA)

2012-2014

Farrell Cunningham (Susanville CA)

Donna Clark (Susanville CA)

Melany Johnson (Westwood CA)

Kenneth Holbrook (Sacramento CA)

Paul Cason (Sacramento CA)

Dan Manning (Greenville CA)

Shiwaya Peck (Greenville CA)
Wilhelmina Ives (Greenville CA)
Marybeth Nevins (Middlebury VT)
Jim Bauman (Washington DC)
Ruth Rouvier (Sacramento CA)

World-Making Stories

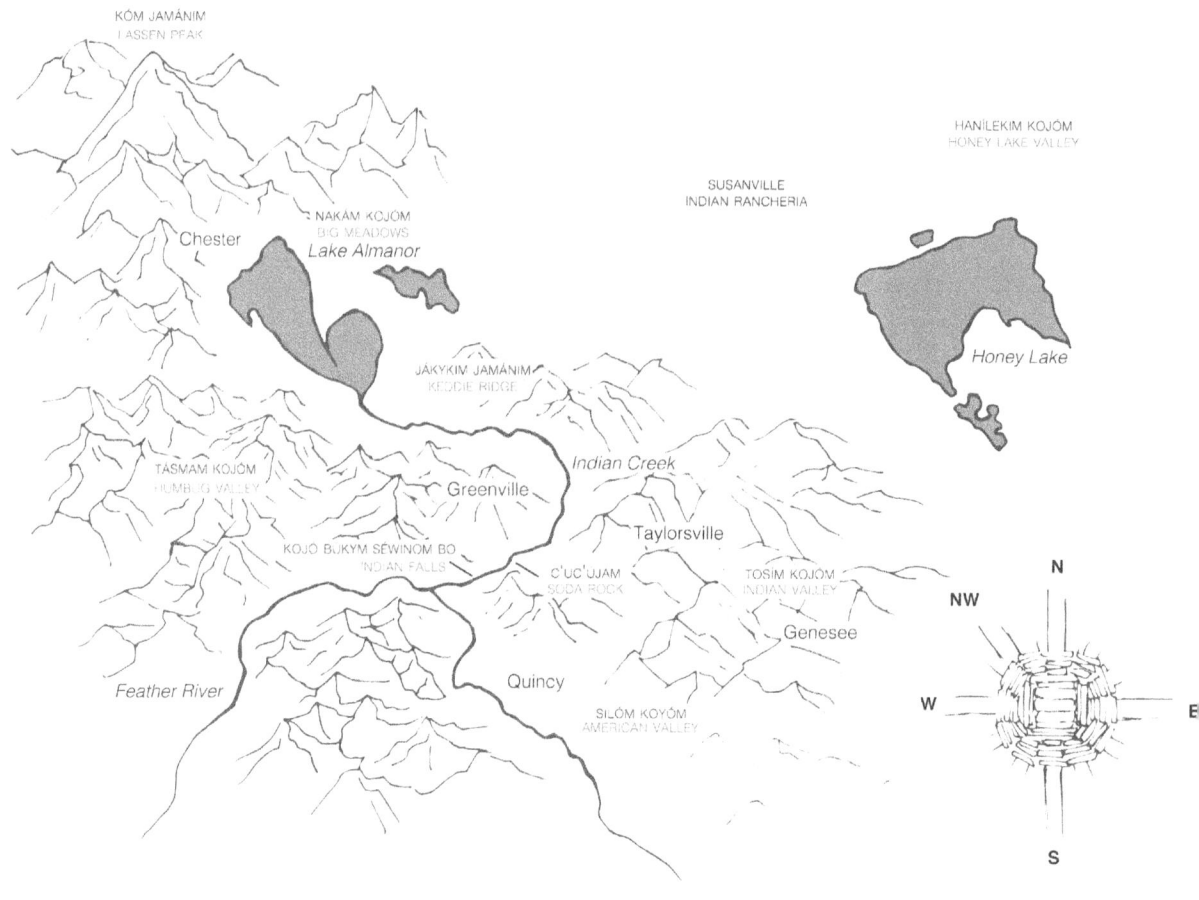

Maidu Places and Stories on a Shared California Landscape. Map created by Weje-ebis (Keep Speaking) Maidu team with support from the Middlebury College Undergraduate Research Office and Digital Liberal Arts Initiative.

Introduction

"Mí unídi bísmaʔamkano," ac'ójʔam.
"Mínk'i k'ódok'an
jakýpem mamáʔamkano," ac'ójʔam.
"Núktim tetémenim k'ódojdi, maʔát
bíswet,
wémt'ikmaʔamkano," ac'ójʔam.

Uním: "Sówonowonos,
amám díwebisim, díwebisim,
hesánbem k'úmmenim wosípdom,
tetét pím k'úmmenim wosípdom,
tetét pím ekím wosípdom,
díbosmaʔamkano," ac'ójʔam.

"Adóm, kaʔámkano díbospem,
púkmapem," ac'ójʔam.
"Anímmyni, mínk'i pekým,
c'ájc'ajnom pekým,
homóbokitmenim pekým, dímak'an;
amýni, kaʔámkano wémt'ik'i húkespem
púkdom,
hónwenumapem," ac'ójʔam.

Awéten,
k'adótkitc'ojʔam.
Awetén, béjby wéjec'ojʔam.
"Mí, béjby, béjby núktim k'ódokypem
mamáʔamkano," ac'ójʔam.
"'Héw! Uním k'ódojnan c'ájnap!'
adóm batásipdom c'ájim kojóna,
batác'ono totomenkym májdym
mamáʔamkano."

"You shall remain here," ac'ójʔam.
"You and your country
will be ones who have names," ac'ójʔam.
"Staying in a country that is little, indeed
not big,
it will be enough for you," ac'ójʔam.

This: "Once I have left,
you will keep growing, keep growing,
how many winters passing,
a great many winters passing,
a great many days passing,
you will have grown enough," ac'ójʔam.

"Then, when you have grown enough,
you shall be born," ac'ójʔam.
"At that time, your food,
different kinds of food,
any kind of food, shall grow;
and you, having been born with enough
intelligence,
shall survive," ac'ójʔam.

Having so done,
he shoved them under the ground, ac'ójʔam.
Having so done, he spoke again, ac'ójʔam.
"You, in turn, will also be ones who have a
small country," ac'ójʔam
"'Hey! Clear out of this country!'
thereby driving others from their valleys,
you shall not become this kind of people."

—Hánc'ibyjim / Tom Young;
ac'ójʔam would translate as "it is said."

CONTINUING RELEVANCE OF "OLD STORIES"
IN NATIVE AMERICAN LANGUAGES

The epigraph with which we begin this preface is part of a longer creation story that was performed in 1902 in Genesee, California, by a man who was known by the names Tom Young and Hánc'ibyjim (pronounced Han-chee-buh-yim). He was well known as a storyteller, raconteur, and ceremonial leader across Maidu and other indigenous northern California networks of his day. He contributed this and other stories and songs to a text collection compiled by Roland Dixon, one of the earliest professionally trained anthropologists in the United States. Dixon was in Genesee under the aegis of the Huntington Expedition to California of the American Museum of Natural History.

California had transferred from Mexican to U.S. jurisdiction only half a century earlier, in 1848, at the conclusion of the Mexican-American War. The document that sealed the transfer, the treaty of Guadalupe Hidalgo, contained provisions for Mexican land rights, but none for indigenous Californians (Middleton 2001, 113). The gold rush followed soon after and brought to Maidu country the single largest mass migration in U.S. history. After treaties brokered in 1850 were hidden away and denied a hearing by Congress, there were no lands set aside for Maidu or other Native American groups in northeastern California. Some lived without the protection of legal title in camps at the margins of settler towns pursuing whatever jobs were available to them. Others lived in mountain meadows, where they continued to tend and harvest acorns and other food plants and to hunt deer, rabbits, and other animals. There were very few protections on their safety and minimal rights of self-representation. Adults and children suffered forced labor, resource depletion, and vigilante violence at the hands of settlers, much of it directly or tacitly supported by the state. The Gold Rush of 1849 occasioned a state-sanctioned killing machine with many participants: cattle ranchers, miner and bounty hunter vigilantes, volunteer state militia, U.S. army soldiers. Killings and kidnappings were in some cases funded by those holding California political office. It is estimated that Native Californians suffered an 85 percent population decline in this period (Middleton 2001, 119; Madley 2016).

According to Middleton, it was the Dawes Act that provided the first limited legal recognition of Native title to California land in its project of assigning allotments to individuals:

> While the allotment or Dawes Act of 1887 harmed large reservation tribes by dissolving their reservations into fractionated landscapes of individu-

ally held allotments, for California Indians the allotments represent one of the few ways in which the federal government recognized California Indian people. Those who are still federally unrecognized today but have an interest in an allotment can show their ancestry back to a person who was recognized individually in order to receive an allotment. (Middleton 2016, 124)

To be sure, only a small portion of those Maidu families dispossessed by the California mass immigration were assigned allotments, but in 1887 the Dawes Act provided an occasion in which some Maidu and other Indian people were involved in conversations with government officials in which they had something to gain from documenting their ancestral occupancy with respect to land. Many Maidu, however, remained outside this process and continued to live without legal title in "Indian camps" (Middleton 2001, 121) and as seasonal migrant laborers. This does not mean that they disappeared or stopped forming distinct social networks. Roundhouses (community houses for ceremonies and visiting) were built out of settler view, and these helped to foster a sense of community across Native Californian communities. Religious movements described as "dream dances" swept through the roundhouses of northern California, as did various forms of native-led grassroots Christianity.

We know that Hánc'ibyjim / Tom Young was a well-known ceremonial leader and master storyteller, but we cannot at present fill in more specifics about his life. It is our hope that this book will inspire those with family stories concerning Tom Young/Hánc'ibyjim to share them in a subsequent publication. The Huntington Scientific Expedition to California ran from 1899 to 1904, one decade after the Dawes Act. Other Maidu people directed Dixon to Tom Young because they knew him to be a cultural authority and to be able to perform a wide array of Maidu stories and songs. Anthropology was still a colonial science, and Dixon was looking to document Maidu language and culture, not as enduring attributes of his fellow citizens but as part of the natural history of California. In the stories performed for him by Tom Young he sought a vestige of precolonial California that he could record for ethnological comparison. It is our conviction that what Tom Young gave him did not directly conflict with these goals but served other purposes as well. Tom Young offered stories that helped Dixon to better imagine K'ódo, the human landscape around them, from before the gold rush, before the brutal trade in young Native "apprentices," before the appropriation of forests for timber and fire-managed meadows for cattle ranches. And Tom Young does something more. His stories also spoke to the still unfolding Maidu-settler re-lations in the northern California landscape around them.

Imagining their research sessions in 1902–3, we can assume that Roland Dixon sat transcribing while Tom Young narrated stories in Maidu language. As he did so, Young gave voice to K'ódojapem, or Worldmaker, speaking to Maidu people at a time before their birth, helping them prepare for that birth by telling them what was to come. Young invites his audience, which includes Dixon, to use their imagination to participate in a sort of time travel. Tom Young (in 1902) intoned K'ódojapem's words spoken by the latter as he pre-pared Young's own ancestors for their life on the land—the same land that surrounded Young and Dixon as they worked together. Addressing these Maidu ancestors before they were born, K'ódojapem told them to expect many things, including a moral difference between themselves and an in-vading people. K'ódojapem modeled for Maidu ancestors the speech of in-vaders, even as he cautioned them against becoming like them " 'Hey! Clear out of this country!' thereby driving others from their valleys, you shall not become this kind of people." The difference between peoples that Tom Young defined in the story extended in obvious ways to the Indian-settler world around the research interview with Dixon and still resonates today.

When we remember Tom Young's position as a spokesman and leader in his community, we can identify at least three arguments in his stories that were not confined to the Maidu past but were also addressed to Dixon and to an audience that includes settlers as well as Maidu. The first argument estab-lishes a prior indigenous moral claim to land. Through "a great many win-ters passing," Maidu ancestors would grow in this place even before being born. Through narrative evocation, repetition, and emphasis, Young asserts for Maidu a strong moral identification with the surrounding countryside be-cause their ancestors have their origins there and have been dwelling there, growing there and staying there ever since.

Second, Young asserts the continued existence for his people in paral-lel and coexistent terms to any other people, including the invading popu-lation. Throughout the story K'ódojapem repeats to Hánc'ibyjim's ancestors that they will have names and that their places will have names. Speaking as K'ódojapem to Dixon and to a broader settler audience, Tom Young thereby asserted the reality of an alternate indigenous way of knowing the world around them, by different names, prior to and alongside the settler world. In doing so Tom Young works against the erasure of native persons and lan-guages that was under way in schools and missions and in the remaking and renaming of the landscape in California at the turn of the twentieth century.

And a third argument is for an environmental ethic of sufficiency. K'ódujapcm tolls Hánc'ibyjim's ancestors that they will have land that is small, not big; but sufficient, providing sufficient food. IIc tolls them that they will be able to live on this land because they will have sufficient intelligence. Having sufficient intelligence to live in a small area contrasts with an opposing mode of action: that of invaders, expanding, taking others' lands by force, taking more than they need for sufficiency while denying to others resources to which they had held prior claim. This was a charged argument in 1902, and it continues to be salient to Maidu and other indigenous struggles for environmental justice and sustainability in California and beyond.

HÁNC'IBYJIM'S / TOM YOUNG'S STORIES TODAY

Someone who recognized the relevance of Hánc'ibyjim's words to ongoing Maidu empowerment efforts and made good use of them was the late Farrell Cunningham, one of the most important Maidu language teachers in recent years. He was also a widely exhibited artist, a poet, an expert in Maidu Traditional Ecological Knowledge, and a founding member of the Weje-ebis Maidu project.

Weje-ebis (Keep Speaking) Jamani Maidu Language Revitalization Project was a documentation and teaching project that was funded by the Administration for Native Americans and administered through the Susanville Indian Rancheria in northeastern California. The project was developed through the tribe's Education and Cultural Resource offices under the directorship of Donna Clark and with help from Cunningham as well as Kenneth Holbrook (Maidu Summit Consortium), Paul Cason (Berry Creek Indian Rancheria), Danny Manning (Greenville Indian Rancheria), Melany Johnson (Susanville Indian Rancheria historic preservation officer), M. Eleanor Nevins (Middlebury College), Jim Bauman (Center for Applied Linguistics), and Ruth Rouvier (UC Berkeley), among others. Weje-ebis Maidu was designed to serve Susanville as well as the broader Maidu language community of northeastern California. In northern California's complex postcolonial landscape, Maidu-identified political networks are spread across eight federally recognized rancherias and a proliferation of other political entities, many of them nonprofit organizations. Many such organizations are associated with prominent Maidu families and devoted to causes such as work on federal recognition cases, land claims, environmental stewardship, health services, and language education (see Middleton 2001, 114–81 for an extensive account). One of the project successes has been to assemble representatives from these organizations in the first intertribal Maidu language summit in the summer of 2013 in Oroville, California. This book is a collaborative effort of the project team.

Prior to helping develop Weje-ebis Maidu, Farrell Cunningham worked for many years with Maidu elders in language and culture discussion groups. He also worked with the U.S. Forest Service and other land management agencies, applying traditional ecological knowledge to forest management. He worked with the National Park Service to develop interpretive materials to help visitors to Maidu country understand the meaning of the landscape to Maidu people. He taught Maidu language classes and from his students we know that he derived lessons in environmental values from Hánc'ibyjim's stories. With his students, he formed a Maidu language theater in Nevada City, California, performing skits about social justice and environmental ethics.

Most important, Cunningham established a philosophical orientation to Maidu language and stories. He defined them not as relics of a departed past but as living potentialities to be discovered and re-created with the ongoing energies of Maidu students and teachers, young and old. For example, Cunningham states (Worldmaker is the vernacular English language translation in Maidu communities for K'ódojapem):

> The places and things of this land are the carriers of the energies involved in Worldmaker's creation. As they are named and expressed in language, they are brought to life. The words and the various components of the land have the power to create and re-create the Maidu perspective each day in a lifetime and during every generation. This is the basis for the conviction that the Maidu people, as a people, were created here in this homeland and that the Maidu language, as a language, was created here as well. (Valborg and Cunningham 2011, 29)

This statement from Cunningham harmonizes with Hánc'ibyjim's words quoted above. As teachers and spokesmen in their communities, Tom Young and Farrell Cunningham invested Maidu voices with the moral authority of long-standing involvement with the landscape as named in the stories while also asserting the relevance of Maidu voices to ongoing public discussions of land, language, environmental justice and sustainability. For our part, the Weje-ebis team invites readers to make connections between the stories presented in this book and ongoing issues concerning Maidu lands and language.

HOW THIS BOOK CAME ABOUT

As part of our work for Weje-ebis Maidu, project director Donna Clark and linguistic consultant M. Eleanor Nevins visited library special collections at the University of Nevada Reno to take stock of their Maidu holdings. One of the project challenges was a lack of accessible Maidu language written materials. The most active teacher of the language, the late Farrell Cunningham, had purposefully avoided writing the language in his classes. Written materials developed through other programs were sparse: a coloring book, alphabet lesson, and word lists. There were Maidu traditional stories taught as part of K–12 cultural education. But these were all in English translation.

Therefore, it came as a surprise when we found Maidu-English bilingual creation narratives in special collections. These were in a set of four oversized linen-bound volumes with Maidu and English lines arranged in parallel verse on facing pages. They were illustrated with hand-carved and painted wood blocks, lithographs, intaglios, and serigraphs. William Shipley was a linguist of long-standing association with the Maidu family of Maym Benner Gallagher and her grandson, Kenneth Holbrook, in Susanville. Shipley is listed as translator/editor, and Daniel Stolpe is listed as the visual artist. A quick Internet search revealed the individual volumes to be available for purchase for $2,350 each, making the entire set a $9,400 purchase. Donna and I both remarked upon how ironic it was that the most elaborate presentation of bilingual Maidu and English texts was published and priced in a form that was outside the means and largely outside the awareness of most tribal libraries and educators, much less the vast majority of Maidu people. While beautifully constructed, the nearly $10,000 cost of the set limited its circulation to well-funded library special collections and private art collections. The bilingual texts are thus not readily available to the broader public and not readily accessible to Maidu community members working in language and culture education.

Still, we immediately recognized the appeal the illustrated stories would have for those working in language and culture education in the broader Maidu community. We contacted the Shipley estate (William Shipley died in 2011) as well as Daniel Stolpe and found that both were eager to republish the illustrated stories in a format conducive to use in Maidu communities and beyond. If we consider the full trajectory from fieldwork with Tom Young and Roland Dixon, through Dixon's and Shipley's publications, this present volume represents the fourth time these stories have been reworked and republished and the first designed with Maidu community use in mind. However, it is worth considering those prior publications and noting that whether packaged as ethno-linguistic data, folklore, or high literary art, the existence of the Maidu community has always been indispensable to the meaning and caché of Hánc'ibyjim's stories for settler audiences.

From his transcripts of fieldwork sessions with Tom Young in Genesee in 1902 and 1903, anthropologist Roland Dixon arranged and published *Maidu Texts* in 1912 as volume 4 of the Publications of the American Ethnological Society under the editorship of the founder of American anthropology, Franz Boas. In the 1912 edition Dixon follows the anthropological conventions of the time in presenting the texts as a series of numbered sentences within block paragraphs, and he provides close interlinear translation for the first story—the creation story excerpted in our epigraph and presented in the main body of this book. This format allowed the texts to serve as sources of linguistic decoding and folkloric studies, but does not convey a sense of the rhetorical or poetic composition of the narratives in Maidu. And further, Dixon's transcription and treatment of Maidu grammar reflect the state of anthropological linguistics in 1912.

The second wave of print publication emerged from William F. Shipley and his work with Maym Benner Gallagher, and later with her grandson, Kenneth Holbrook (who contributes a chapter to this book). Using his more intensive long-term study of Maidu language and aided by advances in linguistics in the years since 1912, Shipley worked with Gallagher to update Dixon's transcription of Maidu language words. In this way they established a bridge between Dixon's earlier work and mid-century American linguistics, between Dixon and Tom Young's work together, and community language revival work today. Shipley was influenced by his participation in Bay Area beat poetry and saw an opportunity in the emerging field of Native American literature for expanding his own work into literature and for garnering public interest in the Maidu texts. To this end Shipley crafted English language literary translations of the Maidu language stories and arranged these in free verse format. He published what he termed a "literary translation" of the stories as *The Maidu Indian Myths and Stories of Hánc'ibyjim* (1991). He enlisted the help of deep ecology poet and essayist Gary Snyder to write the preface, establishing the stories as bioregional literature.

The third publication would come nearly twenty years later, from 2002 to 2005. With artist Daniel Stolpe, Shipley published bilingual English-Maidu editions of the creation narratives in a succession of four volumes, with each page of Maidu text accompanied by Stolpe's illustrations. Stolpe matched the

1. Creation Myth. — Part I.

When this world was filled with water, Earth-Maker floated upon it, kept floating about. Nowhere in the world could he see even a tiny bit of earth. No persons of any kind flew about. He went about in this world, the world itself being invisible, transparent like the sky.

He was troubled. "I wonder how, I wonder where, I wonder in what place, in what country, we shall find a world!" he said. "You are a very strong man, to be thinking of this world," said Coyote. "I am guessing in

Kō'doyapem kan ūniñ' ko'do momim' opit'möni hin-
Earth-Maker   and   this   world   water   full-when

tsetō'yetsoiam.   Hin'tsetoyewē'bisim hōmōñ' kodoi'dimaat
drifted about.   Kept drifting about   where   world-in indeed

nuk'tim kawim'maat tsemen'tsoia. Tsai'tsainom mai'düm
little   earth indeed   saw-not.   Different kinds   people

hesī'kimaat hesim'maat kai'noyemen'tsoia. Amön'ikan
what-of indeed   what indeed   flew-not about.   Then and

5 uniñ' ka'dom tsewu'suktipem ka'dom yotson'otsoia. Epin'-
   this   world   one caused not to   world   he went about.   Above-
                  be seen (?)

iñkoyō'di kō'do tsehē'hetsonopem yak'huböktsoia.
valley in   world   one that looks through,   it felt, seemed like.
                    is transparent

Adōñ'kan wasā' hubök'notsoia. "Hesā'dom ai'tĕ hesā'-
So and   bad   he felt.   "What   I wonder what

dom ai'tĕ hōmōñ' kodoi'di ai'tĕ hesā'pedi ai'tĕ hesā'peñ
I wonder   where   world in   I wonder what (place) I wonder   what
                                                                        at

kodoi'di ko'doi tsehel'ukoañkas," atsoi'am. "Mī kaañ'kano
world in   world   we may see,"   he said.   "You   you are

10 tetet' ep'tim mai'düm amam' uniñ' ko'do huhe'yedom." —
   very   strong   man   that   this   world   thinking of." —

[4]

From "Maidu Texts," Roland Dixon 1912, transcribed from Hánc'ibyjim / Tom Young.
Scanned by M. Eleanor Nevins.

four-volume creation sequence with four print-making techniques roughly in their order of emergence in the history of print. He used woodcuts to illustrate the first volume, *The Creation as the Maidu Told It = pu'ktim* (2002). For the second volume, *The Adversaries =hómpajtotokyc'om* (2003), Stolpe used lithographs. Intaglios were used for the third volume, *Love and Death = hybý'ym masý wónom* (2004). And he used serigraphs to illustrate the fourth volume, *Coyote the Spoiler = wépam wasátykim* (2005).

For this fourth publication of the stories we take up Stolpe's illustrations as well as Shipley's transliterated Maidu language texts. We adapt Shipley's English literary translation, making changes in order to repurpose the stories for use in the Maidu community. Shipley's objective had been to render the stories for non-Maidu English language literary audiences. His English translation departs from the Maidu source text in several respects. With Maidu language revitalization efforts in mind, we have made alternations to Shipley's English translation to make it easier to find correspondences between English translation and Maidu source, sentence by sentence and where possible word by word. For this we returned to Dixon's notebooks and texts to reconstitute the original correspondence where this was lost in the Shipley translation. In doing so we came to realize that there were links between stories, people, and land in the transcript of Tom Young's speech but out of focus in Dixon's ethnological translation and still further obscured in Shipley's literary translation (discussed in chapter 3). Therefore, we made the changes necessary to restore phrase and sentence correspondence and to bring these links between persons and places to the forefront.

This book is the result of more than a century of indigenous research collaborations. Once again we take up the words of Tom Young transcribed by Dixon, transliterated by Shipley, illustrated by Stolpe. We take up these prior publications but require that the English translation defer to the Maidu source. We present them for a new generation to take up, especially Tom Young's heritage community across northeastern California and in their journeys beyond.

AUDIENCES FOR WHOM THIS BOOK IS DESIGNED

Our first purpose is to give members of Maidu and other Native American communities ready access to Maidu oral literature. We have members of the Maidu heritage community in mind as a primary audience. We intend this book to serve as an invitation, an entry point for further cooperative efforts, an incitement to develop other Maidu accounts and arguments. As noted above, we are optimizing the book to serve the goals of language teaching and learning, and to that end we have included previously unpublished guides to reading Maidu written by Shipley. We have also included a glossary of names.

But in addition to optimizing our presentation for language learning and teaching, we also emphasize the moral and political relevance of these stories with respect to Maidu claims to land. They attest to ongoing Maidu presence in the histories of relations among people who have made their lives on a shared landscape alongside one another. Many of the stories describe the origin of particular places, contested places in Tom Young's day. Many of these same places continue to be the subject of argument, cooperation, and political struggle today. And as our opening quotes (to this preface and to the book as a whole) demonstrate, the stories offer a wellspring of opportunities for developing place-based knowledge, educational curricula, and land stewardship. We suggest these points of relevance for contemporary indigenous communities in northern California, but have only scratched the surface. New readers will find connections that we have not. We hope that this will be so.

The second audience we have in mind are residents and visitors to Maidu homelands. For them we hope that this book provides an opportunity to appreciate Maidu and settler California histories and perspectives on landscape that is now under the jurisdiction of public institutions and private industries. The Native American history of the region figures prominently in the economy of northeastern California and bears upon uses of the national forest and interpretive programs of the national park service. It bears upon tourism, logging, mining, and electrical power industries. We hope that this book will be of interest to a broad readership otherwise involved in northeastern California and will provide means of mutual recognition and dialogue on matters of common interest as well as on matters of conflict. This book is an invitation to deepen those discussions.

The third audience we anticipate is a global audience for Native American and indigenous languages, literatures, histories, and ecologies. Maidu community advocacy stands alongside other indigenous empowerment and education projects to name and claim moral relationship with homelands, to recover threatened indigenous languages, and to re-member and reassemble communities in the wake of colonial expropriation. Much of the world-making narrated in these stories concerns land that is now designated national forest or national park. Visitors to Lassen National Park and to national forest land in Plumas and Lassen Counties will find in this book a challenging perspective on what are now U.S. public lands. This is a contribution from the standpoint of a 120-year history of community-academy collaboration. Scholars of science studies, heritage studies, and collaborative community-engaged research will all find arguments of interest in this book.

With this book we attend to indigenous speech that was originally projected across social boundaries in the context of colonial research in 1902. But we show how we can find something more from the speaker in that record than what the researcher may have anticipated.

The texts invite us to understand northern California and United States differently, as a shared landscape that has been implicated in mutual moral involvements (often on unequal, painful, and/or violent terms) across settler and indigenous networks. Telling stories of Kʼódojapem is itself an act of naming and establishing Maidu roles in a long chain of actions that have shaped the northeastern California social landscape.

REPRESENTING THE MAIDU LANGUAGE

See William Shipley's "How to Pronounce Maidu" (chapter 8) for an account of the sounds of Maidu and the transcription system from writing it that we employ for the Maidu language texts in this book.

FURTHER READING

An Act to Provide for the Allotment of Lands in Severalty to Indians on the Various Reservations (General Allotment Act or Dawes Act), Statutes at Large 24, 388–91, NADP Document A1887. Access full transcript at www.ourdocuments.gov/doc .php?doc=50.

Dixon, Ronald B. 1903. "System and Sequence in Maidu Mythology." *Journal of American Folklore* 16 (60): 32–36.

———. 1904. *The Northern Maidu. Bulletin, American Museum of Natural History* 17: 119–346. New York: Knickerbocker Press.

———. 1912. *Maidu Texts.* Publications of the American Ethnological Society. Leyden, Netherlands: E. J. Brill.

Hogeland, Frank L., and Kim Hogeland. 2007. *First Families: A Photographic History of California Indians.* Berkeley: Heyday.

Kroskrity, Paul, and Barbara Meek. 2017. *Engaging Indigenous Publics: Linguistic Anthropology in a Collaborative Key.* Abingdon-on-Thames: Routledge.

Madley, Benjamin. 2016. An American Genocide: The United States and the California Indian Catastrophe. New Haven: Yale University Press.

Middleton, Beth Rose. 2001. "'We Were Here, We Are Here, We Will Always Be Here': A Political Ecology of Healing in Mountain Maidu Country." PhD diss., University of California, Berkeley.

———. 2011. *Trust in the Land: New Directions in Tribal Conservation.* Tucson: University of Arizona Press.

Shipley, William. 1991. *The Maidu Indian Myths and Stories of Hánc'ibyjim*. Foreword by Gary Snyder. Berkeley CA: Heyday.

Smith, Linda Tuhiwai. *Decolonizing Methodologies: Research and Indigenous Peoples*. London: Zed.

Valborg, Helen, and Farrell Cunningham. 2007. "The Mountain Maidu Homeland: Native and Anthropological Interpretations of Cultural Identity." In *Great Basin Rock Art: Archaeological Perspectives*, ed. Angus R. Quinlan, 20–33. Reno: University of Nevada Press.

1

Community Renewal

ONE

This Is Where We Belong

Maidu Histories on a Shared California Landscape

Jesus-im ha'áj kak'án nisé.	Jesus is with us.
Ísk'a, K'ódojapem, uním k'awí,	So, Worldmaker, these lands,
méjwonom.	he gave them to us.
Amádi haj ka'émk'es.	Therefore this is where we belong.
Amá nisé Wólem béj	But White people
Take 'em away jahák'an béj.	want to *take 'em away* from us.

—**Roxie Peconom**

Roxie Peconom was more than one hundred years old in 1956 when she spoke these words (adapted from Shipley 1963, 66–67). Initially reluctant to participate, she had been persuaded by other Maidu elders—Leone Morales, Maym Gallagher, and George Peconom—to gather at the Gallagher home to help linguist William Shipley to document the Maidu language. In this passage, however, Roxie Peconom was doing much more than providing a language sample. Clearly she was also addressing herself to an audience. That audience included members of her own Maidu community, who she refers to as "Ínjánam," which corresponds to the English term "Indians" as well as what she describes as Shipley's community, whom she casts in oppositional terms as "Wólem," which translates as "whites."

In 1902 Roxie Peconom would have been roughly ten years older than Tom Young when he recorded his stories with Roland Dixon. Like Shipley, Dixon would have been Wólem to the Maidu people with whom he worked. Peconom and Young both lived with the difficult legacy of the 1849 gold rush, which had begun on Maidu land and which brought a flood of immigrants and a new era of violence and dispossession into Maidu valleys (Hurtado 1988; Bibby 2004). Her statement fills in a political dimension to Young's stories. She shows that to invoke the name K'ódojapem, which Maidu speakers translate as Worldmaker, in an address to a Wólem researcher on traditional Maidu land was tantamount to invoking long-standing Maidu moral claims of belonging with respect to that land.

In 1902 when Tom Young worked with Roland Dixon, apart from vulnerable individual allotments, there were no lands set aside for Indians in northeast California. Federally managed public lands were established in 1905 and 1907, with Lassen National Forest and Plumas National Forest, respectively. And in 1917, after a series of volcanic eruptions, Lassen Volcanic National Park was established. But there were no lands set aside for California Indians. This changed somewhat in the 1920s in response to the activism of California Indians and the visibility of Indian camps around settler towns and within the newly formed federal public lands. Rancherias were established in northern California to answer the problem of homeless Indians.

[A] large public outcry led Congress and the President to establish 61 small reservations or rancherias, totaling approximately 7,500 acres, for the settlement of homeless Indians. . . . Some of the Indians deemed "homeless" held out and would not move onto the rancherias either, despite being considered illegal "squatters" on National Forest and other public lands. (Goldberg and Champagne 1996 supra note 212:5, as quoted in Middleton 2001, pp. 125–26)

The land set aside was minimal in comparison with reservation territories in other western states: just enough to offer housing, health care, social welfare offices, and other federal services. The rancherias were defined by relation, not to specific ethnolinguistic groups, but to the population of homeless Indians who were living in a given area at the time of their establishment. Susanville Indian Rancheria, for example, incorporates Maidu, Achumewi (Pit River), Paiute, and Washoe residents.

By 1956, when Roxie Peconom launched the verbal salvo with which we began this chapter, termination was becoming a prominent national policy discussion and a looming threat to the rancherias. In 1958 termination was made policy with the California Rancheria Act, Public Law 85–671 (Middleton 2001, 113). Through it, Greenville Rancheria, located in the principal Maidu valley, Tosím Kojóm / Indian Valley, was terminated in 1960 (it was reinstated in 1983, but without land). Roxie Peconom's statement in 1956 can be read as a reflection upon her long experience of settler land expropriation and as an engagement with ongoing political discussions in the 1950s concerning termination and the future status of the rancherias.

SETTLER VS. MAIDU ACCOUNTS OF LANDS AND COMMUNITIES

The gold rush began in 1848 just after the United States' victory in the war with Mexico and just prior to California statehood. Fifty years later, when Dixon worked with Tom Young, he was typical of the anthropologists of his day in his focus on precolonial language and culture. He therefore did not concern himself with Indian accounts of the gold rush and other colonial events affecting their lives. In contrast, by the time Shipley conducted research with Mountain Maidu communities in 1956, linguistics and cultural anthropology had diverged into different disciplines. His purpose was to document Maidu language and to that end he recorded a range of different kinds of speech, including family stories, autobiographical accounts, songs, and conversations. Many of the narratives published in Shipley's Maidu text collection touch on the gold rush and Maidu experiences of settler California, providing a window onto Tom Young's era from the perspective of other Maidu families.

There is still quite a lot of work to be done before we can claim to have broached anything approaching an adequate conversation about what the gold rush has meant to Maidu and other northern California indigenous peoples. We suggest that if read anew with concern for indigenous political voices, some of the personal and family histories in California indigenous language text collections be important moments in that conversation. Dan Williams's account of the gold rush in Shipley's 1963 *Maidu Texts and Dictionary* is a good example:

Wólem Májdem Uním K'ódo 'Ymítdom	**White People Came to This Country**
Wólem májdym uním k'ódo 'ymítdom,	White people came into this country,
'Ínjanà wi'ípem k'ódojdì	crossing over from another country with no
k'ódom'Íynnan,	Indians,
momím jymmotòpem kíwnan 'ysítopindom,	they came over surrounded by water,
'uním k'ódo 'ymítwonòm.	they came to this country.
'Adóm 'uním k'ódo 'ékdadòjkynan,	Coming over into this country from the east,
'yc'ópindom, 'yc'ópindom,	coming over, coming over,
kak'án 'uním k'ódo'éswomìtdom.	they invaded this country.
'Adóm 'Ínjanàm májdym kawónom	And Indian people were living
'uním k'ódi bíspem.	in this country.
'Ínjanàm.	Indians.

'Amá, wóham hadójpem kalétani 'ymítdom,
'amá 'Ínjanàm, jawídom,
"immigrant" 'awónom.

Then, coming in with ox-drawn wagons,
And so Indians, naming them,
called them "immigrant."

'Amám, 'ysítopindom 'uním k'ódo,
Hanílèkim Kojóm 'ysíto
Smoke Creek Nevadadi ysítopindom,
"bó" jawónom kak'án.
Bóm.
'Ánt'ytyt'ym 'ó wokít 'ynódom,
hanysitopìnwonom.
Kak'án wowókinùpem 'ac'éki.
'Amá kak'ás c'ewónom.

So, crossing over hitherto this country,
Crossing over the Honey Lake Valley pass
at Smoke Creek, Nevada,
they made what we call "bó."
A trail.
This size of rock is dropped going along,
carrying [them] across hither.
They are lying there still.
I have seen them.

'Amám, 'yc'ópindom,
Smoke Creek di 'yc'ópindom,
'óm jamáni 'ysítopindom,
Podápem K'ódojdi,
Wipúppùm K'ódojdi 'yc'ópinwonom,
Hanílèkim Kojóna 'éswomìtdom.

Then, coming over,
coming over from Smoke Creek,
coming over from the Rocky Mountains,
coming over from the Bering land,
the Greenland,
they arrived at Honey Lake Valley.

'Amá, mín k'a'ájk'asì.
C'àjìm wónom májdym
nìk'í hònwe pínjahàmyni,
mín japájtodom.

Now, telling you.
If people from elsewhere
want to hear my breath,
to you I am saying this.

'Amám, 'ypìndom,
'uním sèwí, 'uním betém séwwonpinì,
'uním nák'am k'ódonan 'yc'ópindom,
'uním sèwí 'ynnowònom.
'Adóm 'ódo hatámwonòm, 'ódo bádom.

So, coming down
this river, this ancient riverbed,
coming over from this nearby country,
they came down this river.
Then they searched for gold, digging gold.

'Amyni, 'Ínjanàm tawáltiwònom Wóle.
Hójjam Wóle.

Thereafter, the Indians worked for the Whites.
The old-time Whites.

'Adóm Wólem uním k'ódo ymítwonom.
'Adóm uním k'ódo ýpinwonom.
Uním jamánim ýnno,
sewí ýpinwonom.

The Whites came into this country.
They came down into this country.
Coming down these mountains,
they descended the river.

Amádi mac'új?am:
méjtom hybó kywónom.
C'í, damísa sélwonom.

From there mac'új?am:
there was a store there.
They sold clothes, shirts.

Amádi mac'új?am:
nikbék'ym, tawáljat'an
ypíndom;
'ódom dúki, ándykbe ma?at, 'ájk'ate,
mahá?okitdom
nikbék'yjat'am.
Amýni, mym 'ódom dúki Wóle c'etíwonom.

Thereupon mac'új?am:
my father, having previously worked,
came thither;
a sack of gold, about this size, I guess.
Bringing it along with him
my deceased father.
Henceforth, he showed the White that sack
    of gold.

Amýni mac'új?am:
méjdom Wólem,
istówakypem Wólem,
jalálapdojdom,
sýttim kamísa hápdawweten,
ódom dúkini.
Awónom kak'án nikbewk'yjat'am.

Henceforth mac'új?am:
The White trader,
the White storekeeper,
reaching up,
having pulled down one shirt,
gave it, they say, for the bag of gold.
My deceased father told me that.

Amám uním sewí tawál ýpnnowonom,
Adóm, nikbewk'yjat'am.
Amám kíwnan c'ajím májdym
yc'ópinwonom,
Pámwilim májdym.
Amádi kak'án, nikbewk'yjat'am
tawálwonom.
Adóm nikbewk'yjat'am Pánwylim wéje
mákkitwonom.

Then, he worked down along this river,
Then my deceased father.
Then from elsewhere, other people
came in,
Mexican people.
And so, my deceased father
had worked there.
So my deceased father knew how to speak
Spanish.

Adóm "pack train" ak'án nikbewk'yjat'am.
K'a?aj ky?ým ma?ám.
"Pack train, pack animal" ka?ájk'an.
Ka?ájk'as, wéjedom.
Wóleni wéjec'yjdom, "is kinda tangled up"
ak'án Wólem.
Amýni, Ínjanani ka?ájk'as, wéjedom.

My deceased father would say "pack train."
He would do it that way long ago.
He said "pack train, pack animal."
I'm doing it that way now, talking.
His White speech "is kinda tangled up,"
according to the White people.
I am doing it in Indian [to demonstrate],
talking.

Uním séwbonpinim,	This river,
Cariboum sewím piní,	Where this Caribou River comes down,
Sájnem májdym ódo tawálwonom	Chinese people worked gold
Syhýlim séwdi.	on Mosquito River.
Obýnodi unídi,	Here below,
ódo tawáldom,	working gold,
sewí luk'ú píkno tawáldom,	working right in the stream,
ó unína wulútdojwonom.	they started piling gold up.
Amýni, mac'ój?am: líjani, ódo pí hýjewonom.	There, mac'ój?am: they gathered lots of gold nuggets.
Adóm mac'ój?am: tawál'ysipwonom.	Then mac'ój?am: they worked outward.
Adóm uním séwno momí kutídom,	Then damming up the water upstream and
t'úc'ikdom sewí,	draining the river completely,
ódo tawálwonom,	they worked the gold,
wájodom,	tossing
pulúmna wájodom,	tossing into the flume,
wájodom.	tossing.
Sájnem májdym.	Chinese people.
Adóm uním sewí tawál'ýnnowónom, mac'ój?am.	They worked their way down the river, mac'ój?am.
Adóm, mac'ój?am, líjani ódo pí hýjewonom.	So, mac'ój?am, they gathered lots of gold.

In this account (adapted from Shipley 1963, 72–75), Dan Williams integrates personal stories about how a Wólem trader tricked his father, and he goes on to describe the landscape-shaping actions of gold rush immigrants.

Like Peconom, Williams highlights a history of unfair relations between Ínjanam/Indians and Wólem/Whites while addressing an audience that includes both. He says: "Now, telling you. If people from elsewhere want to hear my breath, to you I am saying this." And like Tom Young's Worldmaker stories, Dan Williams also shows how the landscape continues to carry the events that have unfolded upon it. However, whereas Tom Young depicts cosmological events that shaped familiar mountain tops, streams, lakes, and valleys, Williams recounts immigrant movements that carved out trails and placed milestones still visible on the surrounding land.

A further link between Williams's and Young's stories is the fact that both use a variant of the phrase ac'ój?am, 'it is said' (Shipley 1964, 45). Young uses ac'ój?am to mark the end of almost every sentence, or passage, of his creation

stories. By comparison, Williams inflects the word with the prefix "m-" ('they-')
to create "mac'ój?am," a form that translates as 'they say' (Shipley 1964, 31).
Dan Williams makes more sparing use of the construction than Tom Young
does. Williams's first use of mac'ój?am is for a story about how a white trader
tricked his deceased father into exchanging a large quantity of gold for a single
shirt. His second use is for an account of the way that Chinese gold miners
used dams and flumes to extract gold. With "mac'ój?am" he draws upon long-
standing Maidu rhetorical conventions to establish for his audience that these
kinds of stories are widely told in Maidu communities. Looking forward from
the time of his deceased father, or from Maidu witnesses to hydraulic mining
by Chinese immigrants, mac'ój?am establishes these as kinds of events that
people in Maidu communities still talk about and thereby remember.

UNDOING THE COLONIAL WORK OF LANGUAGE DOCUMENTATION AND REPURPOSING RESEARCH FOR COMMUNITIES

It is important to recognize Maidu depictions of the gold rush and other deal-
ings with the settler regime. Their perspectives upon and memories of the
gold rush and other events are part of a continuous indigenous historical practice that continues in Maidu families to this day. They have often gone unrecognized because they occupy a position in the shared indigenous-settler landscape where the general public has been trained not to look. Settler narratives
of Indians doomed to disappear to preclude considerations of indigenous perspectives, emphasizing instead their demise and erasure. The continuation of
"Indian camps" at the outskirts of settler towns and in more rural areas bothered settlers because they imagined Indian communities as only properly belonging to the precolonial past. Of course, as Dan Williams, Roxie Peconom,
and Tom Young show us, the disappearing Indian narrative was not in fact
true. Proceeding as if it were true had the effect of marginalizing indigenous
political voices—because how can anyone be taken seriously in their attempts
to shape the future if they are assumed to only belong in the past?

The notion of the "disappearing Indian" also shaped the young discipline
of anthropology in 1902. Anthropologists saw themselves as salvaging what
was left of precolonial American Indian societies before their inevitable disap-
pearance (Gruber 1970). Dixon's editorial decision to select only "traditional"
genres for inclusion in the text collection reflected anthropological concerns
in 1902. Dixon's purpose was to document and define distinct precolonial languages and cultures. This means that much of the everyday language spoken
around him by Tom Young and others in Genesee and other California settle-

ments was not the focus of his work. Dixon describes Tom Young as fluent in Maidu, Achumewi, and English, but he only included what he recognized as traditional Maidu stories in the published collection. Similarly, stories like Dan Williams' that reflected engagement with settler institutions were almost certainly being told by the Maidu people who worked with Dixon, but such stories do not appear in his text collection.

Dixon's work reflects a defining moment in the establishment of professional American anthropology. He was one of the first graduate students trained by Franz Boas in the first U.S. anthropology department at Columbia University. Dixon followed Boas's linguistic philological model for the documentation of American Indian languages and cultures (Darnell 1990; Bauman and Briggs 2003). To document a set of canonical texts in previously unwritten Native American languages, Boas exhorted his graduate students to use a scientific phonetic alphabet to transcribe spoken stories, songs, prophecies, speeches, and personal accounts in the native language. The usual procedure was to work with bilingual speakers to translate these transcribed texts, word by word, and drilling down into the internal composition of words. Thus transcribed and translated, the native language texts would serve as the raw material for writing grammars and lexicons. Translations of stories, songs, and speeches were taken as cultural evidence and would serve as the basis for ethnological comparison.

In sharp contrast with the present volume, Dixon and other anthropologists did not establish the documentary record with indigenous audiences in mind. Rather, they wrote for academic and governmental audiences. At the time, documenting American Indian languages and cultures went hand in hand with establishing the United States as a modern scientific nation-state. A few larger-scale contexts help to illuminate how this was so. First, Dixon's work was funded by the Huntington Expedition to California of the American Museum of Natural History in New York City (see Swanton's 1902 review). Still foundering in its earliest years, the museum was stabilizing in 1902 under the directorship of financier and philanthropist Morris Ketchum Jesup (Brown 1910). Expeditions to study American Indians established unique content for the new museum and helped garner financial and public support.

The same networks of philanthropists that funded expeditions also funded assimilationist education programs. For his part, Jesup helped to found the Young Men's Christian Association (YMCA) and contributed to other educational and civic organizations whose goals were to provide freedmen and eastern European immigrant laborers with the training necessary to participate in the national workforce and citizenry. The style of training was that of "muscular Christianity," with roots in Protestantism as well as the military (MacLoon 2008). Muscular Christianity seized upon sports, marching, and other techniques for training the body as a basis upon which to train the mind. The assimilationist educational model (Merlan 2009) was picked up for American Indian education via the industrial and mission boarding schools (Lomawaima and McCarty 2006; Reyner and Eder 2006), one of which was established by the Bureau of Indian Affairs at Greenville in 1890. Therefore, in the person of Jesup we find direct links between the scientific investigation of Native Americans and educational institutions designed (with multiple contemporary analogs in the colonial world) to assimilate them to an imagined unitary national standard.

The expedition's benefactor, the late C. P. Huntington, had accumulated his wealth as a shareholder in a California hardware business during the gold rush years. With his associates (including Leland Stanford, who founded Stanford University), Huntington went on to become one of the "big four" behind the Union Pacific and transcontinental railroads (White 2011). Therefore, the Huntington estate's patronage of the expedition realizes direct connections between the anthropological documentation of the indigenous peoples of California and the business enterprises and family fortunes that had grown at the expense of their dispossession.

Dixon's *Maidu Texts*, then, is a product of the formative years of the disciplines of anthropology and linguistics and in the personal networks linking scientific institutions to resource extraction in the West and to assimilation-modeled education for people displaced (through colonization or immigration) by this process. And because of the unique interest in Native Americans among reading publics around the world, early American anthropology enjoyed a distinguished place on the international scientific stage, filling in a missing portion of "the story of man." In the early years of anthropology, the parts assigned to Native Americans in the stories told about them were set in the human past.

However, in documenting Native Americans, the scientists and their political networks were not the only actors on the scene. People like Tom Young, Roxie Peconom, Dan Williams, and Maym Gallagher were equally necessary—indeed, indispensible—to documentation. It is only realistic to expect indigenous contributors to have brought their own purposes to their encounters with scientific researchers. Reflecting upon the nature of the involvement that Maidu and other Indian peoples were afforded in scientific documentation about them raises ethical questions about how indigenous participation in science and civil society has historically been delimited and constrained.

It's worth noting that Dixon was more attentive than many other anthropologists of his time to Tom Young's claims about the history of his own people and their claims about their history with respect to the surrounding land. Dixon and the anthropologist Joseph Swanton came under fire from Robert Lowie for drawing upon oral accounts as evidence in reconstructing indigenous history (Lowie 1915; Swanton and Dixon 1914, discussed in Thomas 2000). In hindsight, the fact that Dixon credited Tom Young's accounts in the face of adverse pressures from his own disciplinary peers is to his credit and can also be partly attributed to the persuasive power of Tom Young and of the other California Indian people with whom Dixon worked.

Therefore, despite its colonial baggage, Dixon and Tom Young's record is valuable to Maidu projects today. Even if Dixon failed to recognize some of Young's meanings (his claims upon the future), the fact that transcripts of Young's stories are included in the public record allows us to return to them with new purposes today. It turns out that, while researchers thought of themselves as documenting an abandoned past, they were in fact establishing an array of texts and recordings that can now be read in new ways, repurposed to other uses, including the political renewal of indigenous communities (McCarty 2013; Nevins 2017; Errington 2008).

MAIDU ON A SHARED LANDSCAPE: KNOWING LAND, WORKING GOLD, AND TELLING STORIES

The statements with which we began this chapter, from Roxie Peconom and Dan Williams in 1956, illustrate the ongoing relevance of Hánc'ibyjim's stories. They show us that moral and political claims to place are expressed through stories. Dan Williams addressed his narrative of the gold rush to a wide audience: "to those . . . who would hear my breath." William Shipley's linguistic text collection includes many other personal accounts of engagements with the post gold rush landscape. These serve as Maidu alternatives and contrasts to settler narratives. With these stories, Maidu speakers emphasize the continuity of Maidu ways of knowing and belonging, even as they grapple with changes to their livelihood and landscape. In the passage below, Maym Benner Gallagher described stories and songs taught to her by her grandparents as her family camped in the mountains and panned for gold. Her account helps us to imagine how Maidu stories and songs have remained on the scene all along in the post–gold rush landscape (adapted from Shipley 1963, 52–53).

Ník'opa	**My Grandfather**
Hójjam k'ódodi,	In the old days,
níktynik'an ník'opa yhéjʔusas	my younger brother and I used to go along
jamánna yk'ójmyni	with my grandfather to the mountain
ódo tawálmamyni.	when he went to work gold.
Pénem níkkotoc'om májc'om yhéjʔusan.	My two grandmothers used to go with us.
Amám jamándi tawáldi ydíknodom	When we got to the gold working place in
kulúmyni,	the mountains,
hybóbe jawéten bej,	and had built a little house,
mym kylókbem	then the old women used to
mahát'usan.	make bread in the evening.
Jahát sá kýweten,	When they had a good fire going,
p'idúsdi maháti jawéten, lýt'usan.	baking it in the ashes, they would bake
	bread.
Amám tawál hékitdom,	When the work was done,
okíthesmyni jahát k'ápdom,	when we came back to camp it was good,
amám tetét jahát dótipe peʔusaʔes.	then we used to eat this very well baked
	bread.
Lýtpem mahátim Wólek'i láwani japém,	Bread baked with White man's flour,
sùdam wasásani síndom,	baked with soda,
bám wasásani sídom,	baked with salt,
tetét jahát dótiʔusan.	used to taste very good.
Nik'opam, ódo tawáldom.	My grandfather, working gold,
Wóleki pilátoni hínnojetidom,	swishing it around in a White man's pan,
awéten nisá mákpapajtiʔusan.	he used to show the two of us how to do it.
Amám tawálhekitbosdsom,	Then, when the work was all done,
amám pebósweten bej,	when we had also finished eating,
nisá tújtiʔusan	they used to put the two of us to bed
Ínjanam hybóbedi.	in the little Indian house.
Amám tújkitbos'esmyni bej,	Everyone would be bedded down,
nisé jáluluni sóltiʔusan,	and he used to play the elderberry flute for us,
tuwéjdom, wéjedom nisé.	praying, and talking to us.
Tetét jahát sóltiʔusan.	He used to play very well.

Éptim wasása nisé wéjemyni,   If he told us scary things,
jyhéptojedom túj?usa?as bej.   we would get frightened and go to sleep.

Amám bej otódom,   Then and getting up
mykáni bej pedóm,   eating the same thing,
béjbym tawálk'ojdom usá?es.   we used to go to work again.

Ka?úsan tetét jahám k'ódodi ynódom,   We would be going along in a very fine country,
pím wasása nisé mákpapajtidom.   teaching us all kinds of things.
K'útt'yt'ym wasása c'edóm: Upon seeing some kind of bird:
"Uním kak'an ka?áwinim,   "This is thus-and-so,
uním kak'an C'istatakym,   this is Robin,
uním kak'an Kájhiskym,"   this is Blue Jay,"
a?únodom,   and so on,
wéjedom niséník'opam.   my grandfather would tell us.
Amám tawálbosweten,   When the work was done,
hybóna ka?émk'es yk'ójmapem.   we would head back home.

—**Maym Benner Gallagher**

Inspiring for Maidu language educators today, Maym Gallagher described her grandparents camping together with their grandchildren, teaching them names of birds and plants, singing songs for them and telling stories.

A NOTE ON TRANSLATION

In the Maidu-English texts that follow, we utilize Shipley's transcription conventions for writing Maidu. This book is made possible by Shipley's well-established scholarship on Maidu phonology and grammar and by his later work translating and publishing Tom Young's stories. However, his goal in publishing Tom Young's stories was to achieve what he termed a "literary translation." This means that he designed an English translation that he hoped would fit the aesthetic expectations of the English language literary audience of his day. Maidu stories were told in a distinct style that shared features with other Native American storytelling traditions, but which were different from the storytelling tradition of the U.S. mainstream. When Maidu stylistic features conflicted with mainstream storytelling aesthetics, Shipley chose to alter the translation to more closely match English. Faithfulness to the poetic and rhetorical form of the Maidu language original was not his top priority, but it must be ours. This is because we design this book to be useful to Maidu language learners and close fidelity to the Maidu original helps readers keep track of the correspondence between original and translation in the bilingual presentation. Another reason we chose to bend the translation closer to the Maidu original is because we are committed to the recognition of Maidu voices, which have been so often obscured in the documentary record precisely because they run counter to mainstream expectations.

Accordingly, we have made some changes to Shipley's English translation where our concern with fidelity to the Maidu source sentences made it necessary to do so. To do this we consulted Roland Dixon's original notebooks and his 1912 *Maidu Texts* because we take this record to be our closest link to the fieldwork dialogue between Tom Young and Dixon. In the few instances in which Shipley's Maidu passages omit portions of the Dixon original, we have restored them. When Shipley added lines that were not present in the Dixon publication, we have omitted them here. When Shipley did not preserve sentence-by-sentence, or line-by-line, correspondence between the Maidu text and the English translation, we have utilized Dixon's publication and notebooks to restore them.

Two changes stand out as especially consequential. We restored passages that evoke, in sun-wise sequence, the cardinal directions to what was the original five direction sequence as documented in Dixon's 1912 text collection. The five direction pattern is explicit, completely regular, and consistent across Dixon's notebooks and in the 1912 publication. Perhaps in an attempt to appeal to the expectations of a wider literary audience (Shipley 1992; Shipley and Stolpe 2000, 2001), Shipley reinterpreted or removed lines of text in order to reduce the five directions to four directions. Following Maidu leaders whom we have consulted, we recognize the importance of the northwest to placing these stories and the people who told them in valleys that share a common northwestern orientation to a prominent peak: Kóm Jamánim. We have used Dixon's notebooks and his original text collection (1912) to restore lines removed by Shipley and to restore the northwest to lines that were either removed or retranslated to other terms. As we will show in the following chapter, this single shift is an act of translational restoration with political, historical, and poetic implications.

Another consequential difference in the present translation is that we, unlike Dixon or Shipley, have chosen to recognize the sentence-final quotative, ac'ój?am, as a structuring element and we represent this in the arrangement of Maidu lines as well as in the English translation. Ac'ój?am translates as 'it is said.' Dixon treated the regular line final repetition of ac'ój?am as a redundancy in the original that did not bear translating after the first sentence in which it occurred. Shipley similarly elects not to translate it. By contrast we, following Hymes (2004), consider the regular repetition of this construction to accomplish important poetic and contextualizing work. On the one hand, it serves as the storytelling genre's most prominent contextualization cue. Using it links Young's storytelling performance to broader indigenous contexts of telling. On the other hand, repetitions of ac'ój?am establish a rhythmic oral unit that we can think of as roughly equivalent to a line of spoken poetry. We are guided by Young's placement of ac'ój?am in our recognition of poetic lines in the story and have used their regular appearance to present Maidu and English lines in correspondence on the printed page.

We have adopted an unusual convention to accommodate ac'ój?am in the English translation. We have chosen to reproduce the Maidu term ac'ój?am at the end of each English language line. We hope that by encountering the term at the end of every line, the reader may always know that we are dealing with a Maidu story and be reminded of the interpersonal spoken status of these stories, as well as their circulation across widespread indigenous communication networks.

PREPARING FOR THE FUTURE: A GOOD AWAKENING

And finally we can think of no better way to end this chapter than with the words of centenarian Roxie Peconom, also from Shipley's 1963 text collection. In this passage, she models how speaking well, living well, and fostering the health of one's community are intertwined. She gifted Mayam Gallagher, Dan Williams, and William Shipley with her prayer, which she attested to using every day (adapted from Shipley 1963, 66–67).

Jaháti Jahám Tújc'eo	I Prepare for a Good Awakening
Kulúmyi, tújdom	When it gets dark, at bedtime
ka?ás túkitdom:	and I am about to sleep:
"Jahám ékdak'oj,	"O beautiful morning,
ník bej yjema'amkano,	you will again come to me,
Hesámenkym k'ódo."	O faultless world."
Amápem kak'ás,	And I say,
"Hésdi ma'at wíjjemenmak'asi," am	"I will not refuse anything," and
"jaháti jahám tújc'eo,	"I prepare for a good awakening,

túj c'enomak'as."   I shall awaken."
A'yjepem kak'ási.   That is what I have always said.

—**Roxie Peconom**

FURTHER READING

Bauer, William J., Jr. 2012. *We Were All Like Migrant Workers Here: Work, Community, and Memory on California's Round Valley Reservation, 1850–1941.* Chapel Hill: University of North Carolina Press.

Bibby, Brian. 2004. *Deeper than Gold: A Guide to Indian Life in the Sierra Foothills.* Berkeley: Heyday.

Dunbar-Ortiz, Roxanne. 2014. *An Indigenous Peoples' History of the United States.* Boston: Beacon Press.

Hurtado, Albert L. 1988. *Indian Survival on the California Frontier.* New Haven: Yale University Press.

Hymes, Dell H. 2004. *"In Vain I Tried to Tell You": Essays in Native American Poetics.* Lincoln: University of Nebraska Press.

Luthin, Herbert W. 2002. *Surviving through the Days: Translations of Native California Stories and Songs.* Berkeley: University of California Press.

Margolin, Malcolm, ed. 1993. *The Way We Lived: California Indian Stories, Songs, and Reminiscences.* Berkeley: Heyday.

Sarris, Greg. 1993. *Keeping Slug Woman Alive: A Holistic Approach to American Indian Texts.* Berkeley: University of California Press.

———. 2013. *Mabel McKay: Weaving the Dream.* Berkeley: University of California Press.

Shipley, William. 1963. *Maidu Texts and Dictionary.* University of California Publications in Linguistics, vol. 33. Berkeley: University of California Press.

Vizenor, Gerald, ed. 1997. *Native American Literature: A Brief Introduction and Anthology.* Longman Literary Mosaic series. Harlow: Longman.

White, Richard. 1998. "The Gold Rush: Consequences and Contingencies." *California History* 77 (1): 42–55.

———. 2011. *Railroaded: The Transcontinentals and the Making of Modern America.* New York: Norton.

TWO

Placing Communities, Languages, and Stories on the Contemporary Landscape

P'únnebisim, betéjtodi,
hesánbem, k'ódojdiwet,
májdyk'i bíspem k'ódojdi,
p'únnemadom p'únc'oj?am.

Knotting many strings, in an ancient time,
for as many lands, in that long ago time,
for as many places where people lived long ago,
he knotted strings in order to send them out,
ac'ój?am.

Májdyk'i bískym t'íkk'ojdi,
hémmamaknoc'oj?am.
Walási hémmakdom p'únc'oj?am.
Awébisim tawálbosc'oj?am.
Awéten: "Sú," ac'ój?am.

The various places where people lived,
he counted them, ac'ój?am.
He counted out the knotted strings, ac'ój?am.
By and by the task was done, ac'ój?am.
And then: "Enough," ac'ój?am.

"Mí ynóp, mym k'ódojdi," ac'ój?am.
"Pok'ók'i hínc'onokydi ynóp," ac'ój?am.
"K'ódom C'ándi ynóp,"
ac'ój?am.
"Májdyk'i bískym t'ik'ójdi ynóp," ac'ój?am.

"You there, go to that country," ac'ój?am.
"Go to the West," ac'ój?am.
"And you others go to the Northwest,"
ac'ój?am.
"Go to where people live," ac'ój?am.

"Mí uním k'ódom Beléwdi ysítop," ac'ój?am.
"Májdyk'i bískym t'ik'ójdi ynóp," ac'ój?am.

"And you go along to the North," ac'ój?am.
"Go to where people live," ac'ój?am.

"Mí uním Ékdadojkydi ynóp," ac'ój?am.
"Uním Pok'ók'i hínk'omónantedi:
uním ekím pok'óm hiná yt'ákym,
k'anájwositodi ynópi," ac'ój?am.
"Wónom májdyk'i bískym k'ódo yt'ájmenwet
ynópada," ac'ój?am.

"You, go this way toward the East," ac'ój?am.
"You, go this way to the South:
where the sun turns to go down,
where it goes straight over," ac'ój?am.
"Go and overlook no place where people
live," ac'ój?am.

Adóm jepónim wéjec'oj?am.
"C'ebó nik'í," ac'ój?am.
"Japájtotok'así," ac'ój?am.

So the leader spoke, ac'ój?am.
"Let them come see me," ac'ój?am.
"I would talk with them," ac'ój?am.

Amýni, yk'ójc'oj?am.
Yk'ójpem, c'ájmen okíkittojec'oj?am.

Then they set off, ac'ój?am.
And going, after a time they returned,
ac'ój?am.

Amám helunini ékdawosipc'et,
myjím k'ódojnak,
ypék'andykbem k'ódojnan okítc'oj?am.
Okíttebisim, okíttebisim,
okítbosc'oj?am.

When only a few days had passed,
from all lands,
people came to that place, ac'ój?am.
They kept arriving, kept arriving,
until all had arrived, ac'ój?am.[1]

FROM THESE VALLEYS, ORIENTED OUTWARD

This passage is excerpted from Hánc'ibyjm's stories (chap. 5, lines 12–23). In this passage Hánc'ibyjim portrays K'ódojapem as he sends out runners to call a gathering of people from villages distributed across a particular landscape. Tom Young sets this passage in the long ago and depicts an indigenous world that is not insular, not isolated, but networked and oriented to the surrounding social landscape. The jepónim, or leader, uses a technique to call an assembly of people that would have been recognizable to some of Hánc'ibyjm's contemporaries in 1903. Taking each direction separately, the jepónim counts out the villages that lay within visiting range—up to several days' journey. He lays out a prepared string for each village and sends runners to distribute these, along with an invitation. To set the day of the gathering and to coordinate runners and prospective visitors so that they gather on the same day, he has tied an identical number of knots in each string: one knot for every day leading up to the planned gathering. Every night his runners untie one knot in their string. When they deliver their message to the invited village, the appointed spokesperson for that village keeps the string and unties one knot per night as she or he prepares for the meeting. In this way each village leader will make their plans with the same destination and the same day in mind.

By Tom Young's day in 1903, sending out runners with knotted string was likely already a remembered, old-time practice. But it continues in other ways. Calling others to a gathering and enlisting nearby allies to help with hosting are aspects of a leadership tradition that stretches from ancestors to the imaginable future. From ancient times onward, the Maidu settlements described by Young were not isolated. Their members kept track of others in the wider world. Sending out runners required knowledge of the social relations on the landscape, extending out to villages within several days' journey. As a renowned storyteller and ceremonial leader, Tom Young himself would have been involved in coordinating gatherings and hosting visitors at ceremonial events in 1903. This passage attests to extended indigenous communication networks that predate settler colonialism and have remained vital alongside colonial networks and continue today. In 1902 something of the same network brought anthropologist Roland Dixon to Tom Young to learn about Maidu precolonial cultural practices and to document stories and songs. In the Maidu community today, there are bear dances, language immersion camps, land stewardship efforts and more, all of which draw upon a tradition of indigenous California networking.

FIVE DIRECTIONS LANDSCAPE

The opening passage for this chapter exemplifies another theme that recurs many times throughout Hánc'ibyjm's stories: space divided into five directions. The leader counts off the names of villages in five directions. This depicts a Maidu world in which people carry in their minds a map of the world that far exceeds their daily paths. It is a map drawn from a center where people live that radiates outward.

Some of the directions, east, south, and west, describe the movement of the sun:

Ékdadojkydi	where the dawn rises	East
Pok'ók'i hínk'omónantedi	where the sun goes across	South
Pok'ók'i hínc'onokydi	where the sun goes over the edge	West

The remaining two directions, northwest and north, point to landforms:

K'ódom C'ándi	at the edge of the [visible] world	Northwest
K'ódom Beléwdi	at the land beside [of that land]	North

To help us understand the significance of the inclusion of the northwest as a cardinal direction, we turn to a statement made in 1999 by a respected Maidu community member, Leonard Lowry.[2] He was the grandson of Suzi Jack, a renowned spiritual leader and healer. He says:

> But very significantly, the Mountain Maidu had five cardinal direction points. They had your north, south, east, west, and then they had northwest. Indian Valley is the hub of the Mountain Maidu, and northwest from Indian Valley is Kum Yamani, Snow Mountain. And then the five is the lucky number for the Mountain Maidu. (Lowry 1999, 80)

Lowry shows how orientation to five directions places the Mountain Maidu in a particular cluster of valleys, with Indian Valley, known as Tosím Koyóm, at the hub. Other major mountain valleys include Nákom Koyóm / Big Meadows (now Lake Almanor), Hanýlekem Kojóm / Honey Lake Valley,[3] Silóm Koyóm / American Valley, and Tásmam Koyóm / Humbug Valley. Northwest to them all is Kóm Jamáni, the tallest mountain visible on the horizon and a recently active volcano.

In this way the five directions in Hánc'ibyjim's stories place the network of people that told, listened to, and learned from these stories in this particular landscape. The settler name for the same mountain is Mt. Lassen, discussed at more length below.

TOSÍDYM

Names: having names and knowing names is one of Hánc'ibyjim's primary themes in the creation story (chap. 4, line 180).

"Mínk'i k'ódok'an jakýpem mamáʔamkano," ac'ójʔam.
"You and your country will have names," it is said.

There is an ongoing discussion among the leaders of language and cultural programs about what name to use within their community for one another. In the ethnological literature, that name is "Maidu." It is used for three geographically adjacent groups speaking related Maiduan language varieties. These include the northeastern Mountain Maidu / Jamáni Maidu (Hánc'ibyjim was identified as belonging to this grouping), the northwestern Konkow Maidu, and the southeastern Nisenan Maidu (Riddell 1978; Golla 2011). Since becoming established in ethnology, the term has been used in governance and passed into common usage. However, there is some criticism within language programs about the use of "Maidu."

Reverend Wilhelmina Ives is a respected traditional elder and religious leader who lives in Greenville, located along Tosím Kojóm / Indian Valley. She served as pastor of the Indian Mission at Greenville for many years and occasionally for Reaching Nations for Christ in Susanville. At ninety-seven years old, Ives has been a leader and educator her entire adult life. She has been language teacher to several Weje-ebis project team members. She argues against using Maidu as a name for the group, explaining that when speaking the language, Maidu, pronounced Májdy, is a basic term for human beings. To specify differences of identity, Májdym needs to be preceded by additional modify-

Kóm Jamáni / Lassen Peak is the white peak in the distance. Tosim Kojóm / Indian Valley is to the right. Photo taken from Arlington Heights by Mark Kidder, reproduced with permission.

ing terms. For example, in Shipley's text collection, Maym Gallagher uses Kóm májdym for "Atsugewi person" and Wólem májdym for "White people," and Dan Williams refers to Ínjanàm májdym for "Indian people," Pámwilìm májdym for "Mexican/español people," and Sájnem májdym for "Chinese people."

To refer to her own people, Wilhelmina Ives suggests Tosídym, which translates as "people of Tosím Koyóm / Indian Valley" (Riddell 1978; Middleton 2001). Danny Manning corroborates that he has heard people from Genesee, American Valley, and Quincy refer to themselves with this term. This makes sense in relation to Lowry's account. Tosím Koyóm stands at the hub of the five directions. Tosídym's local meaning, with respect to Tosim Koyóm, may extend to all the people of the valleys that orient to Tosím Koyóm and who imagine themselves as living parallel to one another via shared orientation to Kóm Jamáni to the northwest. Used in this way, Tosídym would have similar scope to Mountain Maidu / Jamani Maidu, but would anchor that network in place in a particular arrangement of mountain meadows oriented to a particular mountain. Analogous terms for Konkow Maidu or Nisenan Maidu we leave for future discussions. Our purpose is not to settle this matter once and for all but to introduce the discussion and to suggest ways that the five directions in the stories in this volume are relevant to it.

NAMES AND INDIGENOUS COSMOPOLITANISM

Consider K'ódojapem's words in this passage (chap. 4, lines 149–55):

<table>
<tr><td>Wéjec'oj?am.</td><td>He spoke, ac'ój?am.</td></tr>
<tr><td>"Mí mamá?amkano c'ájtikkat wéjepem májdym, c'ájtikc'etípem májdym," ac'ój?am.</td><td>"You shall be people who speak differently, people who appear differently," ac'ój?am.</td></tr>
<tr><td>"Amám, ka?ámkano mí béjby k'ódojkypem mamá?amkano," ac'ój?am.</td><td>"Henceforth, you shall also be people who have a country," ac'ój?am.</td></tr>
<tr><td>"Mínk'i tét'yt'ym, wokódom, ka?án uním kódojnan,
c'áj jákypem k'ódo,
k'ódojdi bísjahadom,
yk'ójdom, bísmapem," ac'ój?am.</td><td>"Your children, growing weary, from this place,
to a place that has a different name,
a place that is good to live in,
will go away and remain there," ac'ój?am.</td></tr>
<tr><td>"Amádi ypék'anim k'ódojdi opítmak'an púkkinudom," ac'ój?am.</td><td>"Being born there, they will live on every bit of the land," ac'ój?am.</td></tr>
<tr><td>Adóm k'an, k'ódo c'etócoj?am.</td><td>And so he divided the lands among them, ac'ój?am.</td></tr>
</table>

C'ájtikkape myná, méjje béjby,	To one giving one sort, and in turn,
sýtti mym k'ódojna mejje:	to another giving a different place:
"Ypék'anim májdym mí kaɁámkano c'áji	"All of you people shall be people who have
jakýpem mamápem."	different names."
Adóm k'an mejje, ac'ójɁam.	And so he gave them all, ac'ójɁam.

Tom Young in 1902 and Lowry from 1920 to 2000 both spoke English as well as Atsugewi and Maidu. They were part of an indigenous cosmopolitan world. Across indigenous California, commanding more than one language was common, as was anticipating how the landscape might be known from more than one perspective and in more than one language. The relative status of Kóm Jamáni is a good example of this. As a prominent peak it defined a border zone between valleys associated with different groups of people and different languages. According to Lowry:

> Kum, that means "snow." Yamani, that's simple. You get variations of how to spell it, but that's phonetic language—it's good enough. That means snow mountain. That mountain was shared also by the Yahi, Yana, you know, Ishi's tribe, and they call it Waganupa, which may be snow mountain, or it might be something else. And then the Atsugewi band of the Pit Rivers had the northern slopes. And they have a name for it; I can't come up with their name, but it means little snow mountain, because to the northwestern corner was the big snow mountain or Mount Shasta, which is much higher. (Lowry 1999, 80)

Kóm Jamáni, then, is a common reference point, but its meaning is anticipated from the divergent perspectives of differently emplaced language groups.

The multilingual, networked quality of indigenous California social landscapes extend through the colonial era. A map drawn by Cora Du Bois depicts the movement of new religious ceremonies across California in the 1870s and 1890s. It conveys a sense of the language diversity and the networked quality of northern Native California (see Du Bois map on facing page).

Although not marked as such on this map, Kóm Jamáni helps to define the boundary lines Du Bois draws. It stands at the northwest corner of Mountain Maidu territory, the southwest corner of Achomawi, and the east/southeast boundary for Yana/Yahi. (Du Bois left Yahi blank because she could find no Yahi individuals to interview in the 1930s.)

Looking at the spread of religious ceremonies helps us imagine indige-

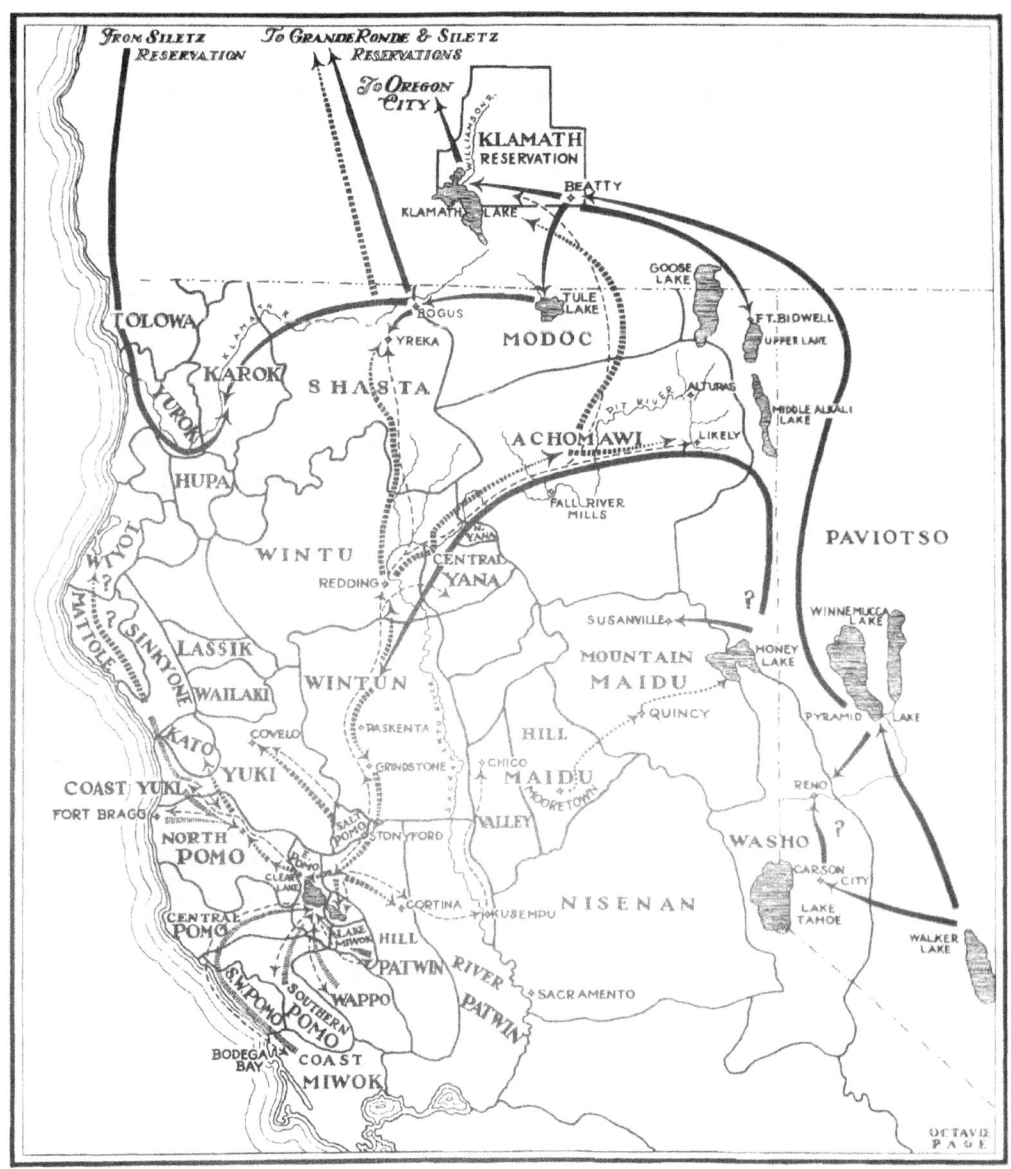

Indigenous networks of northern California from Cora DuBois (1939), *The 1870 Ghost Dance*. Scanned by M. Eleanor Nevins.

nous mobility and widespread communication networks in post–gold rush northern California. The arrows on the map indicate the directional spread of new indigenous religious movements in the 1870s and 1890s, ceremonies which had been named by journalists as "ghost dance" or "dreamer cult." Some of the indigenous testimony in Du Bois's account offers clues to the role of stories like those performed by Hánc'ibyjim at the end of the nineteenth century (see also Seymour 2015). Some of the new ceremonies incorporate ideas encountered from engagement with traveling Pentecostal evangelists. In diverse ways, but like other Christian missionaries, many dreamer prophets claimed to offer control with respect to life after death and prescribed a series of ceremonies and everyday observances to bring about resurrection. Arguments about the dead coming back were more than theological disputes. They were also political. Participation in the new movements often meant repudiating established ceremonies and leadership. When these new religions came through, they were the subject of debate and dispute: taken up by some and rejected by others.

In Du Bois's account, Mountain Maidu were known for rejecting the traveling prophets and aligning instead with established leadership of their own roundhouses. Henry Joseph spoke to Du Bois as a member of another community (Karuk) who had also rejected the new ceremonies. He cited stories about Coyote, very much like Tom Young's stories of Wépam/Coyote in this volume, as his reasons:

> "[A]ll the Indian stories which went way back never had anything in them about the dead coming back. Those stories were like school for the Indians. They told us how things were." . . . [Henry Joseph] then related the tale of Coyote . . . which contained the familiar Californian motif of Coyote ordaining the permanency of death. (Du Bois 1939, 17)

Tom Young's stories can be understood as part of that same history of arguments among indigenous ceremonial leaders. The two principal characters in his stories are K'ódojapem (Worldmaker) and Wépam (Coyote). They cooperate in bringing the world into being from an original watery and indistinct state. But once the world and living beings within it are established, they argue about whether there should be death in the world and whether death should be permanent. The excerpt that opened this chapter depicts K'ódojapem summoning people from the five directions. He does this for the purpose of persuading them to contain and kill Wépam. His claim is that if they do so successfully, death will not be permanent and people will live again after dying. The people then fan out to the five directions, gathering up Wépam's marks on the landscape and capturing him.

In the following excerpt Wépam speaks to them. Here is how he addresses his captors:

Amýni, "Héw," ac'ojʔam.   Then, "Well," ac'ójʔam.
"Ník,   "Me,
mínsym jepónim májdym wónotidom, you leaders of the people are killing me,
mínsy dydýk'ym jepónjahanak'a,"   you would have it that you alone shall lead,"
ac'ójʔam.   ac'ójʔam.

"Níkdyk'y,   "I alone,
ypék'anbem k'ódojnan,   from each and every part of the world,
núkpapajmakyk 'an!" kaʔájcojʔam. will be the one that they laugh at!" ac'ójʔam.

"Adóm, mín"   "And, you,"
—mymým kaʔán—   —turning to Him—
"ypék'anbem k'ódojnak, wasáj amápem: "from everywhere in the world, it will be bad:
'húkeswalawpem!'   'he is the cleverest!'
amák'an mín," ac'ójʔam.   they will say of you," ac'ójʔam.

(chap. 5, lines 110–13)

This quote underscores the political nature of the dispute. We do not know what Hánc'ibyjim's involvement may have been in dialogues among ceremonial leaders of his day. However, the dispute between K'ódojapem and Wépam bears affinities with arguments reflected upon by Henry Joseph between those who hold to the permanence of death as established by Coyote vs. those who follow the possibility of the dead coming back to life. Eventually Coyote slips past his captors and "wins" this argument, although he will suffer the consequences of his own victory later on. Of course, there is no single moral stance to take on this story. Stories like this are taken up differently and made to speak to new circumstances as they emerge.

THE POWER OF NAMING IN A SHARED INDIGENOUS SETTLER LANDSCAPE

Returning to Kóm Jamáni, it is interesting to consider the history of naming this mountain. The settler name is Lassen Peak, after a Danish blacksmith who established the first masonic lodge in the area. He promoted and participated in the 1849 gold rush and was known for blazing a new immigrant trail (which proved to be perilous and was abandoned). He became a rancher in Honey Lake Valley thereafter, where he was killed in 1859 under mysterious circumstances. Despite contravening evidence, public blame was assigned to the Paiutes in the lead-up to what became known as the Paiute wars. In 1861 Lassen's masonic lodge erected a monument to him in Richmond, near Susanville. In 1863 the county was named for him when it was defined as a jurisdiction within the state of California. Lassen Peak was firmed up as the name for the mountain with the U.S. Geological Survey of the same year. Then, more than half a century later, after a series of volcanic eruptions from 1914 to 1920, the mountain and area around it were given the status of Lassen Volcanic National Park.

These official acts of naming emerged from complicated and contested political histories. Their official status plays a role in erasing and obscuring those histories. There are many different community stories to be told about this place, but for our purposes, the name obscures the fact that this is a landscape with a long history of occupation and transformation by California Indian communities. It should be noted that contemporaneous with Peter Lassen's rise to local prominence with the gold rush, a series of treaties were negotiated with assembled representatives (however imperfect) of California Indian groups and submitted to Congress in 1851. Due to political pressure by the new California legislature, none of these treaties were acknowledged or ratified by Congress, and they were taken out of consideration for debate in 1853. This left the majority of indigenous Californians legally homeless. It also left Maiduan peoples invisible on national place-names and maps (Middleton 2001, 170–78).

Naming the national park and mountain for a politically prominent settler was an enactment of colonial relations and an attempt to erase and replace Maidu and other Native California networks, names, and stories. Middleton (2001) argues:

> The great Maidu "nation," if we are to organize people based either on Kroeber's linguistic boundaries, which would include the Nisenan and Concow Maidu, or around the nationalistic views of some Maidu, is one of the largest tribes in California. Yet the Maidu Nation is difficult to find — on a map, in the list of recognized California tribes, and in the census. The reasons for this invisibility stem from the non-ratification of treaties made with Maidu people in 1851, leaving Maidu officially landless. (172)

Maidu names on U.S. maps and lists were confined to esoteric ethnological and linguistic publications during the early twentieth century. However, in the wake of the civil rights movement in the United States and decolonization movements worldwide, this has begun to change. In response to community interests in supporting heritage languages, the Native American Languages Act and the subsequent funding of Native American language documentation and education with the Administration for Native Americans have afforded new opportunities for the expression of Native American voices in California. Collaboration between federal agencies like the Forest Service and the Park Service have made Maidu histories and Maidu-federal partnerships more visible on public lands. For example, the Maidu name for Lassen Peak is featured by the Park Service through the Kohm Yah-mah-nee Visitors Center. Switching between Kohm Yah-mah-nee (Kóm Jamáni) and Mt. Lassen invites park visitors to tack between different histories and different ways of orienting to a shared indigenous and settler landscape.

INTO THE GAP: LANGUAGE, LAND, HISTORICAL AWARENESS, AND COMMUNITY RENEWAL

As Middleton notes, because of the history of nonratified treaties, selective recognition in the allotment era, and the "vagrancy at time of establishment" criteria for enrollment in rancherias, many Maidu persons have not been represented as such within any federal entity. And with enrollments dispersed across ten rancherias, many of which incorporate multiple ethnolinguistic groupings, there is no single entity that represents collective Maidu interests in recovering land and language. Efforts to secure federal recognition for the Honey Lake Maidu have so far been unsuccessful. Into this vacuum nonprofit consortiums, such as the Maidu Stewardship Council, the Maidu Cultural and Development Group, and the Maidu Summit Consortium and Conservancy, have emerged as important community advocates and governance partners. The Maidu Summit Consortium has developed a track record of collaborating with federal agencies in land stewardship and interpretive program development.

As noted by Kenneth Holbrook, director of the Maidu Summit Consortium:

It would be very important not only for our own [Maidu] community to assume a more important role, I think, but [also] for the community at large to really reevaluate the Native community and its value to the overall economic plans of the area up here. We can help develop sustainable tourism: bringing folks in and doing interpretive services for wildlife, landscape, and nature. It's such a beautiful area up here, and there is a real opportunity to reevaluate the importance of the place through perspectives from the Maidu community. So I think that's an opportunity for the entire community up here.

Considering Kóm Jamáni alongside Lassen Peak invites better-informed and pluralistic conversations on national history and our mutual futures on a shared landscape. It is our hope that this book will add to that conversation by providing a counternarrative to the de facto celebration of settler colonialism reflected in the name Lassen. This would be a way to deepen discussions of indigenous-settler histories at this national and international venue.

Many other Maidu families have variations on the stories told by Tom Young to Roland Dixon in 1903. And while these stories are important to Maidu moral claims to the surrounding landscape, they have also become important to the settler community and to tourism development with respect to the copious national forest lands that surround the settler towns of Quincy, Chester, Taylorsville, and Susanville. Many of the events in Hánc'ibyjim's stories correspond to points on the local landscape. The landscape and stories are featured in a road tour promoted by the Indian Valley Chamber of Commerce, Lake Almanor Area Chamber of Commerce, and Plumas County real estate blogs.[4]

The use of Maidu history for tourism development creates a complicated and ambivalent political field around itself. Maidu educators want leaders from their own communities to have a hand in shaping uses of their history in the region. Still Kenneth Holbrook advocates for increased engagement:

I think both communities benefit from taking active steps in bringing together these parties for discussions and dialogue, and finding out what are the mutual benefits of working together, what are the mutual benefits of seeing all of our lands as the shared life resources for people to live up here nowadays in a whole new context. There is a history that calls for greater discussion. The Maidu community has a role to play in all this by learning more about our history and about *their* history. I'm encouraged that Native places have become important to local definitions of place, home, and family. That's what you hope for because when people feel like they're at home, they're going to start taking care of it as if it were home.

And so some of these issues like off-highway vehicle usage—just *rampant* off-highway vehicle usage—you know, over-utilization of "resources"— those issues can be reframed and reconsidered by both parties.

One of the purposes of this book is to add a new educational resource, to provide an occasion for discussion and to invite more Maidu voices into uses of Tosídym/Maidu, or "Indian," stories and names in area tourism.

To contextualize Hánc'ibyjim's stories with respect to their continuing relevance to discussions still taking place among Maidu and settler communities, we point here to a few more of the places featured in the stories, emphasizing overlapping and sometimes conflicting indigenous and settler meanings attached to these places. Many of the places featured in the stories were contested features of a shared indigenous-settler landscape in 1903. Telling these stories to a wider public through the research interview with Dixon expressed a moral claim to place. The stories continue to be relevant to language and cultural renewal because the places that he featured in the stories are still the foci of Maidu and settler politics today. We do not pretend to be exhaustive, only to invite engagement with the stories, the land, and a conversation about shared futures.

JÁKYKIM JAMÁNI / KEDDIE RIDGE 'CANOE MOUNTAIN'

Jákykim Jamáni or Canoe Mountain is the Maidu name for the mountain named Keddie Ridge. It appears as Jakúkim Jamándi in chapter 5, line 282 of Hánc'ibyjim's narratives that follow. Different meanings accrue to the shape of the profile of the ridge. Jákykim Jamani figures the dip in the ridge as the landing place of the canoe after a world flood. The flood was an attempt by K'ódojapem to rid the world of his adversary, Wépam/Coyote, and to disestablish the permanence of death. This is the ridge's textual connection to Hánc'ibyjim's stories. More commonly discussed, however, is an imputed resemblance that this ridge bears to the profiled face of a sleeping Native American man. There are some in the settler community who call this feature "Indian Head." The connotations and politics surrounding the use of that name continue to be ambivalent for Maidu people. By offering long-standing indigenous alternative narratives for the same landscape, we hope to add to the conversation among different stakeholders about this place.

Keddie Ridge is the home of a mountain lake of religious importance for the Maidu community. Homer Lake ("Chom-see-dohm" in Dixon 1905) has

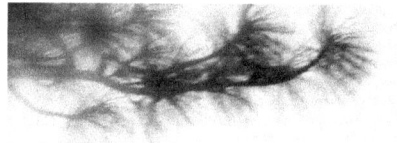

Jákykim Jamáni / Keddie Ridge from Tosím Kojóm / Indian Valley. Photograph by Weje-ebis (Keep Speaking) Maidu team.

been the subject of cooperation between the U.S. Forest Service, rancherias, and Maidu stewardship consortiums on restricting ATV and motorboat access. Donna Clark, Weje-ebis project director, explains:

> Homer Lake is our medicine lake, our power lake, and it is a very sacred place for the Jamáni Maidu. We have been trying to protect it. The forest service—like most forests throughout California and, I'd imagine, the country—are open for recreation, as has been Homer Lake. The Maidu Summit Consortium and the tribes have been working with forestry to make Homer Lake less accessible because it is such a sacred place. We have people that like to go up there and drive their snowmobiles and ATV quads. They leave their garbage; they don't respect the land at all. So we've been trying over the years to make it less accessible to the people for that sort of recreational use. With the forest service we have posted signs on the access roads and blocked roads with trees and boulders to make people walk. The idea is that if people have to pack their things in, they'll pack less and leave less behind. And, in response, the boulders get moved, logs get moved, the cameras set up to catch whoever's moving them get taken.

The stories in this volume fill in part of the Maidu-settler history of Homer Lake. That history is still unfolding today in acts of cooperation between Maidu stakeholders and the U.S. Forest Service. It is also unfolding in conflicts with more destructive forms of recreation in this part of the shared indigenous settler landscape.

CH'ICHÚ'YAM-BAM / SODA ROCK

Like Jákykim Jamáni / Keddie Ridge, Ch'ichúyam-Bam (also spelled C'uc'újam Bom) is a prominent feature that draws Maidu and settler stories to itself. The visual and salt-bearing properties of the water that shaped these formations are connoted in the name which means "urine's trail." Not perceivable in the black-and-white photograph, the predominant color of the rock formation is yellow. Above are hot springs bubbling up through a travertine deposit with warm yellow mineralized water. The enormous stalactite figures at the base formed where the mineralized waters from the travertine deposit run down to the north fork of the Plumas River. Some in the settler community call the formation Dog Rock and say they can see a Saint Bernard or sheepdog face in the contours of the most prominent stalactite cluster. In Maidu stories the stalactites are figured as the remains of dangerous women whose power had

Yellow Stalactites from Hot Springs upslope form Ch'ichúyam-Bam (also spelled
"C'uc'újam Bom") / Soda Rock / Dog Rock. Photograph by Weje-ebis
(Keep Speaking) Maidu team.

to be transformed by Worldmaker as he prepared the world for human beings. Melany Johnson, Susanville Indian Rancheria historic preservation officer, sketched the story like this:

> This is what my family told me, and it could be different with other families. There were three women that lived here. They were witches, bad women, and they didn't want humans to come here. This put them at cross-purposes with Worldmaker, who came in order to bring the people here. He wanted it to be safe for everyone. These women, if they saw anybody go by—as this was in the original story that I learned—they would urinate on them and wash them down. And they would be drowned that way. So there were two animals, I think Mink and Fisher, who were involved in this. Worldmaker told them how to defeat these women. And the women tried to get away. One tried, and she ended up freezing on the stone, so if you look close you can see her body on the C'uc'újam Bom. So that's how Worldmaker made this place safe for us.

In 1902 Tom Young told a variant of this story to Roland. The story associated with this place is the first episode of chapter 7 of part 2, IV: "K'ódojapem Bom / Worldmaker's Trail," lines 2 and 40, where it is spelled C'uc'úje.

After their defeat at the hands of K'ódojapem, the waters in the hot springs above the river became known for their healing power and were visited regularly. The use of this site by Maidu for healing has been disrupted by the development of a travertine mine. The travertine mine on this site was the focus of conflicts among Maidu stakeholders including consortia, tribes, a Maidu mining family, other mining interests, and the U.S. Forest Service (see Middleton 2014). According to Melany Johnson:

> There used to be hot springs up there. I think they are still there but since they disturbed the land they are just really ugly looking. The water used to bubble and it was clean and it was healing. And the old people used to go up there and they would get medicine from the water. And there was also salt grass that went all the way around here. And there is not salt grass anymore.

Access to the quarry site is now restricted due to safety concerns, and federal recognition of the religious and historical significance of the site to Maidu people is marked by its inclusion in the National Registry of Historic Places in 2003.

NÁKAM KOJÓM / BIG MEADOWS / LAKE ALMANOR

Lake Almanor is another example of a landscape feature with compelling Maidu histories associated with it. It was not a lake at all when Tom Young / Hánc'ibyjim performed the stories for Dixon. Young describes this place in his stories as Nákam Kojóm. The name appears in chapter 7, "K'ódojapem Bom," line 46. In Dixon's 1903 account he says that "after Worldmaker slays the dangerous women and other evil beings that would, were they left alive, make life too dangerous for mortal men, he follows upper North Fork of the Feather River, he follows this stream on to Big Meadows" (34).

Until the gold rush, Nákam Kojóm had held long-standing and populous Maidu villages. The Plumas River ran through it. By 1902, when Young and Dixon worked together, the valley was encroached upon by the settler town of Prattville, with Maidu settlements continuing in the margins. Twelve years later, the valley would be flooded as part of the hydroelectrical capture of the Plumas River.

> The area was called Big Meadows, and . . . the little town of Chester is at the northern edge, and of course, Kum Yamani, Mount Lassen, which is a very important mountain to the Maidu, sits to the northwest. . . . Lake Almanor used to be called Big Meadows, and it was called Nacome because of its deep snow, before the PG&E put that dam in there in 1914 that created Lake Almanor. (Leonard Lowry 1999, 80)

It was Great Western Power that built the dam. Pacific Gas and Electric acquired Great Western Power and its associated lands in 1930. "Lake Almanor," the name for that lake that now fills the valley, is testament to the linkage between corporate power, landscape transformation, and place. The name Almanor was derived from the three daughters of the vice president of Great Western Power: *Al*ice, *M*ar*tha* and Elea*nor*.

Lowry described how Maidu, as a result of the 1897 Dawes Act, were first set up with allotments along the lake, an acknowledgment of their prior claim. However, most of the allotments were lost:

> Well, all the Big Meadows bands, of course, were forced out of their place, but most of them retreated either to Indian Valley, or some live around a little town called Chester right now. But then, after the lake was formed, many Maidus took their allotment, Dawes allotment, on the east shore of Lake Almanor. Except for the Baker family and the Salem family, all

Nakóm Kojóm / Big Meadows / Lake Almanor in the foreground with Kóm Jamáni / Lassen Peak in the background. Photograph by Terri Castaneda, reproduced with permission.

the other families sold out. And the east shore right now is just like Lake Tahoe, you know, a summer home for wealthy people.

Some Maidu allotments were lost through the federal powers of eminent domain to make way for hydroelectric development. Others were sold for their Maidu allotees by the Indian agent before the federal twenty-five-year moratorium on resale had elapsed. It is now a developed tourist attraction, and very few Maidu own shorefront property on Lake Almanor, though much of it was once Maidu allotment land.

Melany Johnson puts her ambivalence about the lake as follows: "When I go out here [to Lake Almanor], it's a sacred area, and you know I like the lake. I love the lake. But . . . I wish they wouldn't have done that." She continues:

> Big Meadows: there used to be at least twelve villages, and Big Meadows used to be the largest meadow in California before they turned it into a reservoir. So underneath the water we have village sites. And we also have burials that are in that water. One year in the 1970s the water was so low that our ancestors were showing themselves. So PG&E called in Chico State. They came down and they took everything. Chico State had control and possession of them. Then in 1990 when the NAGPRA law went into effect, universities had to send all their inventories out to all the tribes in the nation. So they had boxes and boxes of our relatives, but they gave them back. We didn't have to go through review committees or anything. They just gave them back. Dr. Greg White was there at the time. So they were returned and reburied at Benner Creek cemetery.

Today under Lake Almanor, Nakám Kojóm / Big Meadows is quite literally a submerged indigenous history. And prior to the Native American Graves Protection and Repatriation Act (NAGPRA), displaced Maidu human remains, like the texts collected by Dixon, were in the archives and labs of universities and out of reach of members of the Maidu heritage community. Now recovery of Maidu language and key cultural narratives is intertwined with reclamation of indigenous persons, histories, and land.

New efforts are under way with the Maidu Summit Consortium and Conservancy to reclaim the names and histories associated with Nakám Kojóm for the Maidu community. Pacific Gas and Electric was forced to divest itself of roughly 140,000 acres as a result of declaring bankruptcy in the wake of energy market deregulation and the ensuing California energy crises of the

1990s. Although admitted to the deliberative process late, the Maidu Summit Consortium has been successful in securing fee title to Humbug Valley / Tasmán Koyóm, which they manage in partnership with the Feather River Land Trust and the California Department of Fish and Game (Spagna 2015). Discussions are under way for assigning the Maidu Summit Consortium fee title to five parcels within the Lake Almanor planning unit, with plans to develop a cultural center on one of these (Middleton 2011, 168–82).

Considering Nákam Kojóm, it's clear that the stories contained in this volume are more than examples of Native American literature. They are also claims of belonging to particular places at a time when there were few means of securing an audience for such claims in the U.S. government or mainstream public. Tom Young planted seeds that today grow into land reclamation, cultural education, and language revitalization.

KOJÓM BÚKYM SÉWINOM BO / INDIAN FALLS

Hánc'ibyjim's stories in this volume end with K'ódojapem attempting "for a last time to try to carry out his promise to men when he made them, that this world should be an easy one, full of pleasure and comfort" (Dixon 1903, 34). One such attempt still visible today is a fishing site that K'ódojapem initially set up right in Tosím Kojóm / Indian Valley so that people living in the villages would not have to travel far to catch a fresh meal. This episode is alluded to in Hánc'ibyjim's stories in chapter 7: K'ódojapem Bom, lines 162–64. In this incident, Wépam has been following K'ódojapem, noting the perfect order he has established, and he determines to make his own mark by upsetting it. Wépam does not destroy K'ódojapem's work but alters it, putting more distance and effort between human beings and what they need in order to live. For the fishing spot this meant moving it to an area that people would have to trudge uphill to visit. And for the sugar pine trees with its low-hanging cones, he moved them out of easy reach so that people would have to climb for their harvest. Pleased with himself, Wépam evokes his relation to Tom Young's audience and to us. He boasts that people shall henceforth tell stories of his cleverness and power. "Then, his work accomplished, he turns his face toward the west, and in his turn disappears" (Dixon 1903, 34).

This fishing site is more widely known today for its waterfall. Indian Falls is now part of Plumas National Forest and is a popular attraction for locals and tourists. Interpretive signage at the site, pictured here, is the result of cooperation between a consortium called the Maidu Stewardship Council and

The Trickster at Work

The ancient Maidu myths that surround the falls started from the beginning of the world. Kodoyakum (Worldmaker) wanted to place the falls in Indian Valley, making it convenient for the villagers to access. Wépam (Coyote, The Trickster), who was always up to mischief, had other ideas, he moved the falls into the narrow canyon where we find it today. While this made fishing more difficult for the Maidu, it serves as a reminder that life is not always easy and we have to work for the things that are most important to us.

Before hydroelectric dams were built in the Feather River Canyon, salmon migrated up Indian Creek. The Maidu used nets, gigs, spears and traps to catch salmon and eel here.

Interpretive signs at Kojóm Búkym Séwinom Bo / Indian Falls evoke Wépam's / Coyote's actions here. Photograph by Weje-ebis (Keep Speaking) Maidu team.

the U.S. Forest Service. Signage features Maidu language names for plants, animals, landscape features, and Maidu stories that are materialized by this particular place.

The Maidu Stewardship Council and Forest Service signs emphasize the Maidu history of this site for both Indian and non-Indian residents and tourists. Much of Maidu traditional homeland is on national forest land, and relations to federal agencies pose new possibilities for democratic participation. From Ken Holbrook, director of Maidu Summit Consortium:

> I think both communities benefit from taking active steps in bringing together these parties for discussions and dialogue, and finding out what are the mutual benefits of working together, what are the mutual benefits of seeing all of our lands as the shared life resources for people to live up here nowadays in a whole new context, in a modern context. And, you know, there's so much common ground. . . . There's a lot of history that needs . . . greater consideration by both of these camps that exist now. I think that the Maidu community has a role to play in all this as well by learning more about *our* history, about *their* history, and then learning about why is it important to a settler family that Maidu places exist. I'm encouraged to hear that this place has become home in a very authentic kind of way. That's what you hope for because when people feel like they're at home, they might start taking care of it as if it were home. And so some of these issues like over-utilization of "resources," you know, those issues can be reframed and reconsidered by both parties.

The stories of Tom Young, Dan Williams, and Maym Gallagher in this volume contribute to ongoing ethical and political conversations concerning public lands.

LISTENING AND LEARNING—NAMES AND STORIES FOR LANGUAGE EDUCATION

So far in this chapter we have focused on the continuing political relevance of Hánc'ibyjim's stories and suggested that moral claims to the Maidu landscape communicated through his stories help motivate participation in Maidu language and culture education. The late Farrell Cunningham proposed that Maidu language and stories have always been a way of seeing and listening to the landscape:

Collaboration between Maidu Stewardship Council and U.S. Forest Service acknowledged on interpretive signs at Kojóm Búkym Séwinom Bo / Indian Falls. Photograph by Weje-ebis (Keep Speaking) Maidu team.

All of the places within the Maidu world that are features recognizable within the creation stories are also places of resources. . . . Within the Maidu world numerous rocks, pools, hilltops, and lakes hold significance as places where the individual may go in order to gain knowledge. Such places, crisscrossing the Maidu homeland, are physical reminders of the world creation. Some of the landmarks, taken collectively, are known as Worldmaker's Trail. . . . The landmarks and features mark the points along this route at which Worldmaker carried out some world preparatory action. Each of these landmarks contains a story of its creation. (Valborg and Cunningham 2007, 30)

Going to these places to listen and gain knowledge is a practice involving personal and environmental cultivation. Keith Basso describes a parallel practice among the Apache people with whom he worked (Basso 1996), and Lisa Brooks (2008) argues for the importance of recognizing narratives, naming, and other indigenous place-making practices to the recovery of native space.

Cunningham treats Maidu words for places, plants, and animal species. He examines the meaningful internal composition of these names and identifies what they reveal of an "implicit ecosystem understanding" among Maidu ancestors (Valborg and Cunningham 2007, 29). These include words such as watkym (mallard), bybým ch'ám (a species of pine tree), and C'uc'újam Ba (a rock formation also known as Soda Rock). In each case the meaningful composition of the word reflects a quality of that plant or animal species that was important to how Maidu persons have experienced and drawn a living from their homeland. We follow Farrell Cunningham in this respect and invite readers to listen to the stories in the names. The glossary of names at the back of the book is designed to support this possibility as well.

Finally, we close this chapter with a place-making invitation from Dan Williams, which he performed for Maym Gallagher and William Shipley in 1956. It was published as part of Shipley's 1963 *Maidu Texts and Dictionary*. He provides a fitting guide to how Hánc'ibyjim's / Tom Young's stories and the Maidu landscapes of northeast California might be attended to.

Ník Wónom Májdym Ník Hiníswopajta

Nisém ka'ʔémk'es epínim kojódi,
kaʔémk'es jahám k'ódojdi bísmapem,
wónomenkym májdym wónomenkym
k'ódojdi.

Let Mortal People Catch a Glimpse of Me

We shall be in heaven,
we shall dwell in good country,
immortal men in an immortal
land.

Amám, wónodom,
wóno?yk'ojmanimmyni,
kak'án mín, uním banákpem banákpem
hybóm,
uním k'a?ásk'ojkym púlkym.
Amápem k'a?ásk'ojdom.
Amádi, ka?ámkano mydí ysítomapem,
wóno?yk'ojdom.

So then, dying,
when you will depart in death,
for you, this bright bright
house,
this opening door will open.
There you will cross over.
In this way, traveling as a spirit.

Adóm, ysítodom,
c'ehéjhejk'ojnimmyni,
ka?án jóm,
banákdojdom,
jokácipem jóm.

Then, crossing over,
as you look about you,
there are flowers,
brightening,
(untranslated), flowers.

Ejádom býwomyni,
ejádom býwowok'ojmyni,
jahám k'ódom
wónomenkym k'ódojdi amápem, a?ám.

When the wind blew in this manner,
when the wind passed by in this manner,
a good country
in an immortal land came into being, a?ám.

Adóm kak'án K'ódojapem májdym,
K'ódojapem kak'án ka?ájwonom,
uním k'ódo púktidom.
Adóm, uním jamáni,
teténomon jamáni,
óm jamáni, bysýpkitdom.
Momí hekít?yt'ojwonom,
k'ódom bodíknokydi,
bétejtodi, k'ódo yk'ókdom.

Then it was Worldmaker person,
Worldmaker who spoke in ancient times,
bringing this world into being.
And so, these mountains,
these many great mountains,
stone mountains, laying them down.
He went along,
putting down into place the waters,
in ancient times, moving over the country.

Adóm uním Helám Púksakym
Jamáni,
mym Paním Bisím Jamáni mak'án,
mym Béldynim wosípippinim jamáni.

Then he made the Grass-Game Creating
Mountain,
this Tobacco Dwelling Mountain,
this mountain just a little further up from
Beldon.

Amánan ynódom,
Amím Jokólt'anum Jamáni mawónom.

Going from there,
he made that Flag-On-top Mountain.

Cariboum bówoc'onom by?ás wodójno.
Amánan yk'ójdom Papájdi ymítdom,

Going a little further along the Caribou trail.
Getting to Papájfi,

Sihápkym woc'ónodi,
bénkitwonom.
Solóm kak'án c'etípem.
Uním bénsitodom,
bénkitwonom.

onto the vicinity of Sihápky,
he put down his foot.
The footprint is visible.
From there stepping across,
he put down his foot.

Áweten, amánam yk'ójdom,
ysítodom Eltúdasim henántedi,
Eltúdasim wodójnom jamánnodi:
"Uním matá,
uní ka, ký?ym ma?ás, K'ódojapem.
Amám, ník wónom májdym ník
hiníswopajta.
Adóm k'ódom jákymamyni,
kak'ás myn símpanim,
kak'ás púppupmapem," ac'ój?am.

Thereupon, going from there,
crossing this side of Alturas,
along in the mountains beyond Alturas:
"Let this be,
this did I, Worldmaker, create long ago.
Therefore, let mortal people catch a glimpse
of me.
So when the land is overcast with clouds,
it is my beard,
it is becoming gray," ac'ój?am.

"Amét, k'ódom jahámamyni,
ypé jahádom kak'ás,
unínan c'esítomapem,
k'ódo c'ánna c'esítonumapem."

"Then, if the land fares well,
when the weather is good,
I shall look across from here,
gazing steadily northwestwards."

Kaním kak'án.

Done.

NOTES

1. In this passage and others we have utilized Shipley's transliteration of Dixon's Maidu texts, but have reconstructed a translation of the Maidu words and sentences from Dixon's (1912) when Shipley's literary translations departs too radically from the original Maidu spoken text. We have also followed Hymes (1981) in arranging the stories into spoken lines, marked by the line-final particle ac'ój?am.

2. Born in 1920 and raised in Susanville, California, Lowry's heritage included Mountain Maidu, Washoe, and Hammawi Pit River. His grandmother, Suzi Jack, was a traditional Maidu doctor. His mother was a linguist. He had a distinguished career in the military and, prior to that, in the civilian conservation core.

3. The late Dan Williams told William Shipley (personal communication 1995) that Hanylekim was a Maidu name for the lake and that the English name is a corrupted borrowing from Maidu. According to Shipley (personal communication 1995), it could mean something like "carrying something quickly along." From http://www.honeylakemaidu.org.

4. http://indianvalleychamber.snappages.com/An%20Ancient%20Trail%20-%20A %20Maidu%20Auto%20Tour.htm; http://lakealmanorarea.com/scenicghistorical

gtours.htm; http://www.sellingplumascounty.com/canyongdamggreenvillegindiang andggeneseegvalley/.

FURTHER READING

Basso, Keith. 1996. *Wisdom Sits in Places: Landscape and Language among the Western Apache.* Tucson: University of Arizona Press.

Dixon, Ronald B. 1903. "System and Sequence in Maidu Mythology." *Journal of American Folklore* 16 (60): 32–36.

———. 1904. *The Northern Maidu.* Huntington California Expedition. *Bulletin, American Museum of Natural History* 17: 119–346. New York: Knickerbocker Press.

———. 1911. "Maidu." In *Handbook of American Indian Languages*, 1:679–734. Bureau of American Ethnology, Bulletin 40. Washington DC: Government Printing Office.

———. 1912. *Maidu Texts.* Leyden, Netherlands: E. J. Brill.

Golla, Victor. 2011. *California Indian Languages.* Berkeley: University of California Press.

Hinton, Leanne. 1994. *Flutes of Fire: Essays on California Indian Languages.* Berkeley: Heyday.

Lowry, Leonard. 1999. (Interviewed in 1993 by Helen Blue). Cathleen Coles, ed., University of Nevada Oral History Program. http://contentdm.library.unr.edu /cdm/compoundobject/collection/unohp/id/2503/rec/15.

Middleton, Beth Rose. 2001. "'We Were Here, We Are Here, We Will Always Be Here': A Political Ecology of Healing in Mountain Maidu Country." PhD diss., University of California, Berkeley.

———. 2011. *Trust in the Land: New Directions in Tribal Conservation.* Tucson: University of Arizona Press.

———. 2014. "ChuChuYamBa / Soda Rock: Toward an Applied Critical Geographic Perspective on Traditional Cultural Properties (TCPs)." *Human Geography* 7 (2).

———. 2015. "Jahát Jatítotòdom": Toward an Indigenous Political Ecology." In *International Handbook of Political Ecology*, ed. Raymond L. Bryant, 561–76. Northhampton MA: Edward Elgar.

Riddell, Francis A. 1978. "Maidu and Konkow." In *Handbook of North American Indians*, vol. 8, *California*, ed. Robert F. Heizer, 370–86. Washington DC: Smithsonian Institution.

Spagna, Ana Maria. 2015. "A Displaced Tribe Reclaims Sacred Land: The Mountain Maidu Return to Their Valley, but the Work of Reclamation Never Ends." *High Country News*, September 14, 2015.

THREE

Wéjenim Bíspadà

A Brief History of Maidu Language Keepers and Other Thoughts on Language Revitalization

Kenneth Holbrook

The purpose of this chapter is to share a history of some of the central figures of Maidu language revitalization during the past 120 years and to pay tribute to their dedication. I also introduce some ideas about the variety of Maidu language work accomplished during this period, which I hope will inspire the reader to assume his or her handle on the oar we all pull together.

There have surely been other projects not cited in this brief summary that have yielded many works of much importance. For Maidu readers, if you would like to share the work of a language keeper, we invite you to do so via the Maidu Summit Consortium website (http://www.maidusummit.org /home.html). All past and present efforts made in the direction of the on-going language renaissance among the Maidu people are respectfully invited and acknowledged and I feel should be celebrated with lasting applause and support. Wéjeʔebìs!

LIVE BY THE LANGUAGE

On the wall of the Maidu Summit Consortium, a mural designed by the late Farrell Cunningham reads: "May these sacred and aboriginal words you share never be forgotten!" Farrell inspired many elders and young people alike with his artwork and his philosophical approach to teaching Maidu language in concert with extending Maidu environmental stewardship with respect to traditional Maidu lands. His mural at the consortium expresses an idea with many components to explore. Sacred? That's a start. What is sacred about a language that now lives on the lips of so few, those who can be counted on two hands? What does knowing this language mean for the Maidu people, the people who so graciously gave me life and now call me kin? Yes, even some of our Maidu people at times scoff at the spiritual significance that others attribute to knowing one's tribal language. Or how about the word *aboriginal*? Does this mean the language literally derives from the place where its speakers, recent Maidu ancestors, lived at the time of contact with European settlers?

I continually ask myself these questions because the mantra offers so much to ponder. "May these sacred and aboriginal words you share never be forgotten!" I suppose it teaches the entire Maidu and settler descendant community a lesson. When we do not understand the aboriginal people of any given place, we eventually lose a knowledge base and set of practices. We lose aboriginal perspectives on how to live sustainably in place over the long term. Therefore, that Maidu and other aboriginal languages should "never be forgotten" is of a piece with a set of values in which place-based knowledge is held in high esteem. For many in the Maidu community, understanding our language provides us with a connection to the place-based knowledge of our grandparents and great-grandparents. At least this is true for me. As a Maidu man I feel compelled to solve the riddle because of the innate and powerful duty to learn and teach Maidu language, which I have felt since I was nineteen years old. The work has been both a blessing and a challenge.

Perhaps for the multitudes of so-called conquerors, the real goal in contemporary language revitalization work is the very same idea that began back in the late nineteenth century at a national strategic level: documentation for science. We should collect and catalog the vast array of cultures and languages of the Indians, as explained in ethnographies, song and story recordings, and grammar descriptions developed by academic experts, archived, and subsequently made available for presentation as featured items in American museums, libraries, special collections, and ongoing academic research for the indefinite future.

By this, it was thought, Americans will respectfully but effectively put to bed one of the touchiest of all subjects in our nation's history: the unrelenting and systematic extermination of the life ways of the aboriginal peoples. The extermination of Native American languages was furthered by a punishing policy of English language assimilation during the nineteenth and early twentieth centuries. The children of the original inhabitants of this country were kidnapped and then subjected to the cruel Mission School system in order to learn how to dress and act as the settlers deemed appropriate. They were also beaten without sympathy if ever they spoke their native language while in captivity. As the U.S. government implemented policies that effected the eradication of each tribe's language, somehow it also saw fit to support efforts to send out experts to document what they hoped would soon be a relic of a bygone way of life. To me, what they have documented are actually the still relevant words and wisdom of my grandparents.

This work involved Roland Burrage Dixon, a graduate student of anthropology at Harvard. A young man of privilege and an aspiring protégé of Franz Boas, Dixon worked with a Maidu speaker beginning in 1898 as part of a project directed by the American Museum of Natural History. The ethnolinguistic documentation of Maidu would later involve a highly regarded linguist of his day. This was William Shipley, or as my family knew him, Bill. Bill was a Berkeley-trained linguist and a distinguished student of Mary Haas. He worked for more than fifty years with my great-grandmother, Maym Benner Gallagher, communicating to my family his respect for the Maidu and all indigenous peoples. I knew him to be dedicated to the cause of promoting Maidu language use in the community.

At first glance, it is easy to see why some folks from my community have been severe in their disapproval of the various documentary works pursued by Bill and other academics. Because their very purpose of collecting language data was seen as yet another thinly veiled extraction of a valuable resource from an impoverished community, the attitude has grown for some that the work created was inherently bad.

In fact, there have been a number of occasions throughout the years when members of our own community were the ones aggressively seeking termination of Maidu teaching efforts in response to the vocal disapproval of a few. A deep-seated emotional response is natural when discussion arises about an ideal future for the Maidu people and their drowning language. Clearly there have been those who felt that we must keep the little that we still know to ourselves, as individuals, sheltered from outside researchers and institutions.

This might be the story for some, but as for the Maidu people whom I have spoken to in recent years, a very different initiative has emerged. We feel that the most important reason why we must never forget the words of our grandfathers and our grandmothers is simple: wisdom. No one will achieve wisdom without knowing the rhythms and cadences of our mother tongue and without hearing the poetry of our ancestors. Without an ear for singing along with the other creatures of our Maidu world, Májdym K'ódo. Their songs are our songs.

That is why each day I wéjenim bíspadà. In English, this would mean something like "live with the language" or "live by the language." By this I mean to remember to think in Maidu as much as possible. I do my best to imagine new ways of using my aboriginal words: to reflect upon life or to talk to the robin who lives in my front yard, whom I greet each morning as I take my children to school. My daughter has lovingly dubbed this robin Beaky, whereas I call her C'ístatàky, which is the Maidu way, often quietly and to myself. By doing so I give thanks for the profound blessing of my having been granted the chance to learn the real word for "robin."

But let's take our inquiry a step further. Why has the revitalization of Maidu, one of the indigenous peoples of California, a population that has experienced widespread linguistic decimation, actually been able to enjoy some progress in revitalizing efforts in recent times? While many other neighboring tribes have struggled to achieve similar goals, the Maidu have leveraged critical information made possible by the determination of a few forward-thinkers.

From a Maidu point of view, dubious circumstances allowed for the numerous collections to be expropriated over the years for academic purposes, either knowingly or unknowingly, by folks like Dixon, Shipley, and Dorothy Hill. One can become skeptical of the merit of such works as being useful for the Maidu today. The differences in cultural perspective of the parties involved in various language recording efforts played a distorting role in what they produced.

On the other hand, there are also many detractors from our own community who are guilty of having thrown the proverbial baby out with the bathwater due to understandable bias and distrust. All of this, of course, has evolved out of a larger context of an unrelenting and expedient cultural assimilation of Native Americans. By adding it all up, one might easily conclude that these and many other factors should have dashed all hopes of rekindling our language generations ago.

Might it be that buried beneath all the naysaying and misdeeds, there can be found an even greater truth? Maybe it is with the precious few who faced their critics head-on with whom we should place all our thanks and to whom we should dedicate all our ongoing work. By this I mean the Maidu language contributors and language teachers, its keepers.

My feeling is that a greater story is found when considering the lives and contributions of the Maidu who persevered in speaking the language, singing the songs, teaching the names, and telling the stories even as they came face to face with the very pressures that have led to language shift among so many others. The era of assimilation and removal, the subsequent generations of cultural upheaval, and what would become the fallout of a divided community—these are the perils that continue to threaten the sustained use of Maidu language. These were the circumstances that folks like Hánc'iby?ìm faced in 1902.

It is my purpose in the following pages to explore these heroic agents of Maidu language survival: its keepers, to whom I give all my appreciation and humble thanks for their tireless work and heartfelt passion in the face of over-whelming challenges. As time marches on, we shall come to know what is in store for the Maidu language and for its people. Regardless of how our story unwinds, my hope is that we never forget our sacred and aboriginal words and that we will always celebrate those who secured them as forever ours, against the odds.

It is my intention to briefly summarize the life and works of each of the following Maidu people, as related to the history of Maidu language survival. My hope is to continue exploring the lives of these important Maidu leaders in future works.

Due to my own family's extensive collections and oral history providing me with vivid details and an ample supply of accounts of her many years of language work with Bill Shipley, I am able to offer more on the subject of my great-grandmother, Maym Hannah Gallagher. Any disproportion of historical material presented here, based on subject, is merely a result of that.

HÁNC'IBY'ÌM (TOM YOUNG)

Tom Young was the name given to Hánc'iby'ìm, the accomplished and re-vered storyteller from Genesee, California. He was a Maidu/Atsugewi man in his twenties when he decided to contribute what he knew along with his ar-ray of musical talents. Today one can still listen to the song recordings that he made as Dixon implemented the technology of the time: wax cylinder phono-graphs. Imagine it. Recordings of a Maidu storyteller from the late 1800s! This is the treasure we now enjoy because of the important decision that Hánc'iby'ìm made. He opted not to withhold what he knew, as many have done, but rather to allow its recording.

For this we owe so much of the success that Maidu has enjoyed when considering the efforts of others. We are so blessed to have a long legacy of Maidu language keepers. The creation story recounted in this book describes the coming of the world, as understood by a traditional Maidu storyteller schooled since youth by the elders of his day. This ancestral voice, sharing his story of our beginnings, grants us a lasting spiritual and cultural echo to guide us home.

Regardless of the antiquated national agendas that led to the "capturing of our language," as I have heard it put, I continue to cherish the results. Were it not for the various initiatives that led folks into the field to record Maidu, we would have little to work with today. I wish that were the case for more tribes.

This is certainly true of the Hánc'iby'ìm recordings. Roland Dixon, a man with a severe and demanding personality, was not in Maidu country in 1898 to serve our needs as the grandchildren of a socially wounded and culturally affected people. Little thought was given to the value that his work would hold for a linguistic stock to rekindle their fire with generations down the road. His mission was aligned with the larger scheme of agencies and foundations of that era to box up and put away the relics of Indian cultures. Ironically I sense that the digitized copies of the original wax cylinder recordings that share with me the voice of Tom Young are of little help to anyone except a contemporary Maidu seeking to learn more of the language. In this way, one must prefer these extractive research campaigns to the actions of the Spanish bishops who chose to burn the Mayan codices.

Hánc'iby²ìm grants us a literary legacy that is entirely our own. His contribution to the revitalization of Maidu is profound. It provides us with a basis from which we discern the long-standing resonance of all works produced since that time. It is how we know that the work done by the contributors that would come years later holds merit. To him, we as Maidu learners today owe a tremendous debt of gratitude.

MAYM HANNAH GALLAGHER

Ever since the mid-1960s Maym Gallagher has been a name synonymous with Maidu language. She was known by her own kin as "Mamie." By all accounts, and even aside from family history, it seems fair to paint my grandmother as intelligent, witty, sophisticated, and far ahead of her time. I have no recollection of my own, as she passed away when I was only six months old.

It was in 1954 when a thirty-three-year-old graduate student from Berkeley showed up at my grandparents' place near Payne's Creek, California. William Shipley was that student. He and a colleague were out searching for my family based on a recommendation from Fritz Riddell, a longtime family friend and highly regarded anthropologist. My great-grandmother, Lena Thomas Benner, agreed to let them record her pronouncing words in Maidu. My grandmother, Maym, who was in her sixties at the time, was to be alongside her to stand by in support. Everything worked out just fine.

This process was pleasant for all, and a plan was formed to continue the work in the coming months. As Bill became more familiar with the scenario at my family's home, he realized that it was Maym who would be the ideal language contributor, as she was fluent in both Maidu and English. This would become even more apparent to him as the next few years of work unfolded. Bill never failed to attribute so much of his success in scholarship to my grandmother's capacity to discern what it was that he was up to. "She seems to possess an innate understanding of the nuances of my work as she was being introduced to the concepts involved," he recalled. "It was truly remarkable! She was just brilliant."

Of course I relished the opportunity to have a glimpse of my grandmother outside of the families' own memories. A vast amount of energy and time were given by Maym and Bill to achieve the priceless work that would eventually be published as the *Maidu Text and Dictionary* (Shipley 1963). It is because of my strong desire to carry on to the best of my abilities the legacy she has left that I share with my children the words of their grandmothers. They will never be forgotten.

HERB YOUNG

Tom Young's son, Herb, was a major contributor as a Maidu language keeper. During the 1960s and 1970s, Young spent countless hours producing the voluminous Herb Young Audio Recording Collection, which was directed by Dorothy Hill of Chico, California. Herb shared in his father's love and talent for storytelling and singing.

Young was born in Genesee in 1892. Raised by the famed basket weaver Selena Jackson, Herb was surrounded by traditional cultural practices throughout his life. His recording series is relished for its array of information, spanning from linguistic, to historical, to traditional methodologies and the changes they incurred throughout his life. This collection represents a vast series of Maidu stories, personal recollections, Maidu vocabulary, as well as tribal and family history.

Just as his father's work offers us a glimpse at Maidu as it was in 1898, it is important to also place the material that Herb Young provides along the timeline of Maidu language revitalization into the 1970s. In our efforts to maintain the sound, cadence, and authenticity of our language, we look to our elders who took the time and made the effort to record what they knew.

LILLY BAKER

A name less often associated with Maidu language revitalization is Lilly Baker. Known universally as the most celebrated Maidu basket weaver of the twentieth century, she also spent years quietly promoting Maidu language. By teaching a young Farrell Cunningham all the Maidu language she could recall, she performed a heroic service to her people.

The time spent with Mrs. Baker afforded Farrell so many doors into the Maidu world because she taught him the natural words spoken there. As days passed, he appreciated ever more the music of our language, the inter-pretations of life in Maidu country and beyond, which you will only gather by using the proper language. This is what he would tell me.

Baker's role in the continuing saga of Maidu language resurgence was one of giving. She chose to do this work by sharing her knowledge with the younger generation in a time when it was uncommon to do so. Just as we have so many thanks for the work Farrell did for our community in language and traditional ecological knowledge renewal, we must also give thanks to Lilly for her unwavering commitment to passing on the beauty of Maidu to Farrell.

VIRGIL LOGAN

Virgil Logan, who still resides in Oroville, California, has committed his life to doing any work he can to recall the Maidu he learned from his mother as a child and to teach it to the next generation. His work became focused on his father's language, Konkow Maidu, which is a closely related language of the neighboring tribe. However, through the course of our work on the current project, Weje-ebis: Yamani Maidu Language Revitalization Project, Logan has devoted a tremendous amount of time to recording. He seeks to reassert sev-eral phonetic attributes of Maidu that were distinctive to him as he listened to his mother speaking to him. "I didn't like the way some folks taught it be-cause they don't pronounce it right," he used to lament. To this end, he has recorded multitudes of proper word pronunciation into digital files for use by future learners. It has been a great joy to become his friend.

TOMMY MERINO

Tommy Merino was universally known throughout our community as a lan-guage teacher. He led statewide efforts to improve educational opportunities for Native Americans, founding the California Indians Educational Associa-tion and serving as its president. He taught Maidu language classes at D-Q University in Davis, where he also served on the board of education. He also taught Maidu language classes at Susanville Indian Rancheria and spent de-cades doing what he felt was best for our community.

Although this period did not yield much in the way of rekindling wide-spread language usage, it was an important phase in which a familiarity with

Maidu sounds was maintained with a few folks who would come and recite the word lists they worked from in his classes. There is no question that much good came of Tommy Merino's dedication and years of service to aid in language learning.

This particular piece of the story is a difficult one for me to recall. Merino was certainly one who advocated for language revitalization, but he also stymied the very same efforts made by others on several occasions. Unfortunately, I was in attendance when one of these occasions occurred.

In 1997 I had traveled to the town of Oroville, California, to attend the first Maidu Language Summit, which was staged at Mooretown Rancheria. Virgil Logan was attending that day, and so were several other Maidu leaders, including Tommy.

My mentor, Bill Shipley, had been invited to deliver a keynote address to an audience that he hoped would find inspiration in the work he and I were doing at the time. We had been working on a new dictionary that would be useful to language learners. We had applied for a grant to do the work, which we would be awarded from the Endangered Languages Fund of Yale University.

Tommy interrupted Bill's talk and instead wanted to discuss how he felt the language Bill was teaching me was somehow not Maidu. The exchange became heated, as Tommy took issue with Bill's Maidu dictionary work and with Bill's authority to teach the language. His criticism was due in part to a misunderstanding arising from differences between the format and organization of Bill Shipley's dictionary and that of popular desk companion dictionaries. In fact, the dictionary was laid out in a way that can make it difficult for most readers to understand. Instead of a vast collection of word occurrences, as in the case of an English dictionary, the data is organized by word roots. This is an unfamiliar approach to most Maidu, since we are all native speakers of English and have had experience with popular alphabetical dictionaries of English.

The sad outcome of that day was Bill storming out of a gathering, which he had traveled many hours to attend. It was one of those occasions you wish you could forget. Bill and I would work on our own over the next six years and attempt to introduce the fruits of that labor for use in the community. The path to Maidu language revitalization was never going to be an easy one to find. Fortunately, allies were abundant, and it was only a matter of finding them. Today it feels like a much more inclusive attitude prevails when it comes to Maidu people supporting each other in their work.

There is no question that Merino was a champion for the cause of the Maidu people. He fought bravely to defend his community and the United States as a decorated veteran of foreign wars.

A number of years would transpire before I could glean any more from the encounter between Tommy and Bill that day in Oroville. My distaste for the way my mentor was treated was all that I could see. It also hurt me to assume that by my academic association with Bill, I may have been perceived by a few as an agent of an imagined cultural transgression by laboring in my studies. The vision of creating something to offer my community as a language reference tool seemed positive to me.

My strong instinct at the time was to continue to do the work and be available to any student when the right time came. I am now very happy this was the case and that good fortune provided the opportunity. However, I would also come to have a more evolved sense of the importance of the events at the Maidu Language Summit. It would be years before I could understand exactly what it was that prompted the public opposition to Bill Shipley's attempt to make his linguistic publications relevant to the community. But I was nineteen, and I had much to learn.

FARRELL CUNNINGHAM

My dear friend Farrell Cunningham, with whom I shared so many years of collective interest and collaborative work in Maidu language revitalization, passed beyond our world in the late summer of 2013. He and I were working together on our respective portions of this book and many other efforts toward Maidu language when Kʼódojapem chose for his journey home to begin. He was thirty-seven years old.

The very first thought I have when recalling Farrell is the boundless love he had for speaking and teaching Maidu. His immense joy in speaking what he called the "real language" was so plainly apparent to anyone in his company whenever he obliged. He felt that it was his duty to share his ability to speak the language with the few Maidu who remain. In fact, Farrell embodied the very spirit of Wéjenim Bíspada. To say that Farrell was a catalyst for the regeneration or, better stated, the repatriation of Maidu language would be an understatement.

I myself learned Maidu within a purely academic setting, by way of literature made using our stories in the Maidu oral tradition, collected nearly 120 years ago and at various other stages of time since then. This was a very different approach from that of Farrell, who enjoyed the great fortune of having access to speakers as a boy. I enjoyed the process of learning historical linguistics and phonology and considering the various ideas which linguistics had yielded to that point.

The difference in our respective learning environments meant that Farrell and I had to do some work in order to understand how our knowledge could cohere. My initial objective for learning Maidu language was for the purpose of teaching it to others, just as I had learned it. As time would pass, I would develop a deep appreciation for the basis of Farrell's way of learning Maidu by repetition of spontaneous discussions shared among family and friends. This provided him with a different set of skills but also a different set of challenges, vis-à-vis the state of our nearly moribund language. Some years would transpire before we would accept each other as the counterparts into which we had grown. More than this, Farrell and I would come to love the nature of our respective approaches to learning and teaching Maidu. He and I understood the intrinsic value of his spontaneous use of everyday language in daily settings and my capacity for understanding the workings of the Maidu language linguistically. Together we planned to provide prospective language learners with a new curriculum and vibrant instruction that was solely created of, for, and by the Maidu people.

As a young man in his Greenville community, Farrell began participating in Tommy Merino's classes, but found that he disagreed with Merino's teaching method, which was based on the repetition of word lists. Farrell decided to teach his own Maidu classes, drawing upon fluency he had achieved under tutelage with Lilly Baker and Wilhelmina Ives. His classes received some support and participants, but were largely muted by the continued protestations, based on a sense of being circumnavigated and thus disrespected by his elder, Merino.

Farrell's frustration with his community being insulated from new and innovative ways to cultivate a resurgence of Maidu speakers intensified as years went by. He decided not to confront his elders by continuing his instruction in Maidu country. He respected them. Instead, he ended up in the village of North San Juan, California, where he would come to live within a community of artists on an outlying private property in the forest for some years. It was here that he would find tremendous success in teaching the language (see Anderson 2014).

He recalled that perhaps as many as fifty students matriculated his program with varied success. His approach of teaching the language orally with little to no attention given to writing or standardization of orthography and pronunciation, which had been taking place concurrently within project trips back in the traditional Maidu homeland, granted him freedom to delve into cultural arts in a much more tangible way. The nature of the community where he stayed allowed for the sort of participation required to achieve rapid gains. Days were spent rehearsing skits and performances that were given exclusively in Maidu language. Critically important ideas of social and environmental justice developed from his language class using stage performance as their vehicle to gain conversational fluency.

For a time, this scenario rewarded Farrell with a belief that it was possible for his own people to truly recapture the use of Maidu in their everyday lives. He also realized that he must reacquaint himself with the community of his people and bring his teachings back to the Maidu, where they would find a home within the Weje-ebis project at Susanville.

We spent the final year of his life traveling around to the many homes of the elders we still knew to speak even small remnants of the language. Folks like Wilhelmina Ives, Ruth Peck, Andrew Jackson, Shiwaya Peck, Beverly Ogle, Taras Gaither, Franklin Mullen, Dorothy Miles, Alfred Kitchen, Nola Bowen, Hazel Beatty, and Virgil Logan would all become participants in our goal of researching all that is still known to be shared among the last few speakers of Maidu.

At the same time, we also drove to remote corners of traditional Maidu homelands to document the Maidu world using photography and hand-written notes, along with corresponding audio recordings of the appropriate Maidu words and phrases associated with the images and writings.

This process never concluded, as Farrell journeyed before our work was done in Májdym K'ódo. I trust that he is presently singing, laughing, and praying with his beloved elders in Epínim K'ódo, calmly waiting for the rest of his Maidu kin to join him in the ancient gathering.

LIVE WITH THE LANGUAGE

The work presented in this volume has proudly been assembled for the purpose of your having access to the story of creation, written just as it was told by our Maidu grandfather, Hánc'iby?ìm. First collected sometime around 1898, it has been reassembled to include all minutia originally contained for historical accuracy and in spiritual recognition of the importance of this work. It is presented bilingually with the corresponding English translation appearing on the opposing page.

This story originates in the iron-rich soil of Plumas and Lassen Counties, in the salty flats of the Susanville Basin and the crystal-blue and frigid spring waters of Tásmam Kojó, where my family lived. It is from where your family started. We all share in the significance of this masterpiece.

Eloquently told by Hánc'iby²ìm, of Yatómatom Kojó or Genesee Valley, this original tale describes our creation and vividly recalls the numerous episodes between K'ódojapem and Wépam Wájsi, also known as Earthmaker and Coyote, that prompted the birth of our world, all its creatures both human and otherwise, grasses, plants, and trees, technologies and customs, and above all a codex of morality that is singularly Maidu, aboriginal in every sense of the word.

For me, there is no question about the spiritual significance of learning my ancestral language. By living with the language, I have found immense joy and reassurance. Learning a little language every chance I get is extremely rewarding in this sense. My hope is that others feel the same need.

What a precious gift that time has given us. May we honor the work done by the individuals spoken of in this brief history of language revitalization work and remember the years of their lives that they dedicated to the cause we carry on today. Without the link they provided between Hánc'iby²ìm and readers today, we would have little hope of continuing to echo among our mountains the song of Maidu.

Whatever the purpose which has delivered you to this book, may you find within it the inspiration I have in reading of the birth of our culture, of our people, of this world, and of the story of each new day, as it is eternally reborn with the dawn of morning sunlight.

Héw wỳnnaj.

Dedicated to the lasting legacy of my great-grandmother, Maym Hannah Gallagher, and to my adopted grandfather and dear friend, Bill Shipley.

FURTHER READING

Anderson, Karen Lahaie. 2014. *Mountain Maidu Grammar*. Self-published.

Dorothy Hill Collection at CSU Chico. Manuscript 160 Audio, photos, and transcriptions for Herb Young: http://www.csuchico.edu/special-collections/documents/MSS%20160%20Guide.

Eargle, Dolan H., Jr. 2007. *Native California: An Introductory Guide to the Original People from Earliest to Modern Times*. San Francisco: Trees Company Press. (Discusses Tommy Merino.)

Lomawaima, Tsianina K., and Teresa L. McCarty. 2006. *To Remain an Indian: Lessons in Democracy from a Century of Native American Education*. New York: Teachers College Press.

Riddell, Francis A. 1978. "Maidu and Konkow." In *Handbook of North American Indians*, vol. 8, *California*, ed. Robert F. Heizer, 370–86. Washington DC: Smithsonian Institution.

Shipley, William F. 1963. *Maidu Texts and Dictionary*. University of California Publications in Linguistics, vol. 33. Berkeley: University of California Press.

Spack, Ruth. 2002. *America's Second Tongue: American Indian Education and the Ownership of English, 1860–1900*. Lincoln: University of Nebraska Press.

UC Berkeley Survey of California and Other Indian Languages (Shipley's materials are all here in audio). Francis Riddell's collection and also Maidu songs recorded in 1911 with Ishi: http://www.linguistics.berkeley.edu/Survey/.

2

Creation Narratives of
Hánc'ibyjim / Tom Young

FOUR

Púktim / Creation

Púktim	Creation
K'awí c'epém májdym	Earth-seeing person
tetét ek'áwpintidom solí	very beautiful songs
betéjtom solí	ancient songs
sólpem Májdym	song-singing person
Pénem húk'espem májdyc'om	Two wise persons to one another
uním k'ódo jamádom	making this world
húsemwetewdom	talking it out together
hesíwet maʔát wasánupe c'edóm	seeing indeed anything that is bad
jahátimaʔamkano, ac'ójʔam.	making it good, ac'ójʔam.

K'ódojapem k'an,
uním k'ódo momím opítmyni,
hínc'etojec'ojʔam.

It was Worldmaker who,
when this world was covered with water,
floated and looked about, ac'ójʔam.

Hínc'etojewebisim,
homóm k'ódojdi maʔát,
núktim k'awí maʔát,
c'eménc'ojʔam.

As he floated and looked about him,
indeed any land,
indeed even a tiny bit of earth,
he did not see, ac'ójʔam.

C'ájc'ajnom májdym, hesík'i maʔát,
hesím maʔát,
kájnojemenc'ojʔ am.

Any different kinds of people, indeed any,
indeed any kind,
none were floating about, ac'ójʔam.

Amýnik'an, uním k'ódo c'ewúsuktipem,
k'ódo jýc'onoc'ojʔam.

And so then, trying to see this world,
he went along in the world, ac'ójʔam.

Epínim kojódi, k'ódo c'ehéjhejc'onopem;
jákhybykc'ojʔam.

An open sky-meadow, a see-through world;
it was just like that, ac'ójʔam. (5)

Adóm k'an, wasáhybýkc'ojʔam.
"Hesádom, ájte;

And then, he felt bad, ac'ójʔam.
"Where, I wonder;

Woodcut by Daniel Stolpe.

heśadom, ájte;

homóm k'ódojdi, ájte;

hesápedi, ájte;

hesápem k'ódojdi kódo

c'eheluka?amk'as?" ac'ój?am—

—mym kak'án mymyk'í epínpem.

"Mí ka?ámkano tetet éptim májdym,

amám uním k'ódo húhejjedom:

homónnantem k'ódojdi k'ódom ujákk'en

amá húpaj?" ac'ój?am.

"Anímmyni amám k'ódojdi híntatapy?y,"

ac'ój?am.

"Uním k'ódojdi

hínc'etojewebisim,

hínc'etojewebisim,

ókdom, hesí ma?át peméndom;

okó wónomaky?amkano," ac'ój?am.

Amýnik'an húhejjec'oj?am.

"Wíjjek'así," ac'ój?am.

"Hesí ma?át hút'amenk'así," ac'ój?am.

"Héw!" ac'ój?am.

"K'ódom kak'án tetém, tetém k'ódom,"

ac'ój?am.

"Esápediwet, núkti ma?át k'ódo

c'edóm,

jahánac'ehasí," ac'ój?am.

Awéten k'an, sólc'oj?am.

"Homóndi, núktim k'ódom, uk'á?" ac'ój?am.

Sóldom, májc'oj?am.

Sólwebisim, ypék'ani sólwebisim,

"sú," ac'ój?am.

Sólhekitc'oj?am.

"Héw! Hesándykbe ma?át solí

mákkitmenpem kak'ás," ac'ój?am—

Wépam.

where, I wonder;

in which world, I wonder;

where, I wonder;

in what sort of place

might we two see a bit of land?" ac'ój?am—

—this is what he asked.

"You are a very powerful person,

to be thinking up this world:

which side of the world do you guess might

have some land?" ac'ój?am.

"So that we might float there to that very

place," ac'ój?am.

"If in this world we go

floating and looking about,

floating and looking about,

hungry, but indeed not eating anything;

I fear we may die of hunger," ac'ój?am. (10)

And so then he thought, ac'ój?am.

"I don't know," ac'ój?am.

"Indeed, I cannot think of anything," ac'ój?am.

"Well!" ac'ój?am.

"The world is very big, a big world,"

ac'ój?am. (15)

"If somewhere I find a world that is, indeed,

small,

I will make something good of it," ac'ój?am.

And accordingly, he sang, ac'ój?am.

"Where, little world, are you?" ac'ój?am.

He said it, singing, ac'ój?am.

Kept singing, kept singing until,

"Enough!" ac'ój?am. (20)

He stopped singing, ac'ój?am.

"Well! Indeed there are not many songs

that I don't know," ac'ój?am—this was

Coyote.

Woodcut by Daniel Stolpe.

Awéten k'an, mymým bej sólc'oj?am.
Sólwebisim, k'ódo epíndom, sóldom:
"Homóm k'ódojdı, k'ódom, uk'á?" ac'ój?am.
Sólc'oj?am.
Sólwebisim "Sú!" ac'ój?am.
"Wokók'as. Mí béjim mákwonop!" ac'ój?am.

Amýni k'an, K'ódojapem sólc'oj?am.
"Hesák'a?" ac'ój?am.
"Nik'í tetém jamánmantom?" ac'ój?am.
"Nik'í k'ódom jamánmantom," ac'ój?am.
"Hesák'a?" ac'ój?am—weyebisim.
Sólhekitc'oj?am.
"Sú!" ac'ój?am.
"Mík'un kýdawe," ac'ój?am.

Mákc'oj?am—sólwebisim.
"Nik'í t'íwkym jamánmanto,
k'ódom jynókydi," ac'ój?am.
"Héw! Tetét ha?aj hesí ma?át
c'eménmaka?amk'as homóm k'ódojdi,
k'ódom uménjákk'en,
áj sy?ýj," ac'ój?am.

"Núktim k'ódo, áj sy?ýj, c'edom,
tetét jahánac'e?as," ac'ój?am.

Hínc'etojewebism, k'an
t'ut'úm jákkanupe c'ec'oj?am.

Adóm k'an, "Héw! Tetèt ha?áj tibík'an,"
ac'ój?am.
"Núkti tetébe udóm, jahánac'en,"
ac'ój?am.
"Amét núkti tibík'an," ac'ój?am.
"Hesátidom, ájte,
núkti wi?áswajtonac'ehasí?" ac'ój?am.
"Hesáti jahá?" ac'ój?am.

And so, after that he sang again, ac'ój?am,
Kept on singing, singing for land:
"In what world, land, are you?" ac'ój?am.
He sang, ac'ój?am. (25)
He kept singing until "Enough!" ac'ój?am.
"I'm tired. You try again!" ac'ój?am.

And so then Worldmaker sang, ac'ój?am.
"Where are you?" ac'ój?am.
"My great mountain ranges?" ac'ój?am. (30)
"Mountains of my world," ac'ój?am.
"Where are you?" ac'ój?am—he kept saying.
He stopped singing, ac'ój?am.
"Enough!" ac'ój?am.
"You try," ac'ój?am. (35)

He tried, ac'ój?am—kept singing.
"Misty mountain ranges,
place where one can go about," ac'ój?am.
"Well! If indeed we two
shall not see any at all,
then such a place may not exist in the world,
I think," ac'ój?am.

"If a little world, I think, I could find,
it would be very good," ac'ój?am.

Kept floating along, and
they found something just like a nest,
ac'ój?am. (40)

And then, "Well! It really is small,"
ac'ój?am.
"It would be good if it were a little bigger,"
ac'ój?am.
"But it is really small," ac'ój?am.
"What can I do, I wonder,
to stretch a small thing out?" ac'ój?am.
"What would be good to do?" ac'ój?am. (45)

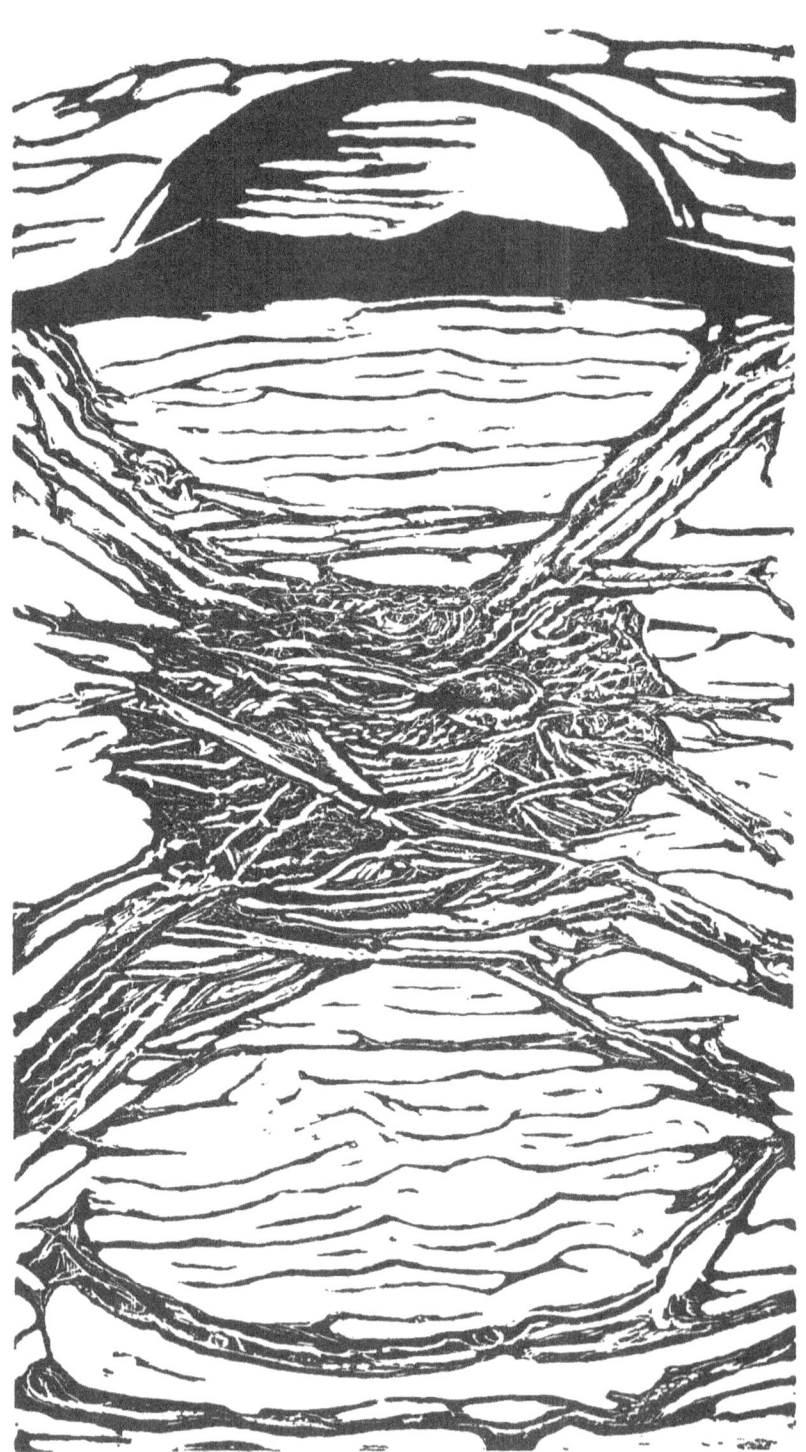

Woodcut by Daniel Stolpe.

"Hesátidom tetébewti mak'áde?"
awébisim k'an, sikésc'oj?am.
Píwbok 'ojtic'oj?am.

"In what way can I make it a little bigger?"
and as he talked, he transformed it, ac'ój?am.
He stretched it out, ac'ój?am.

Ékdadojkydi, píwbok'ojtic'oj?am.
Komódi, píwbok'ojtic'oj?am.
Kok'ók'i kýc'onokydi, píwbok'ojtic'oj?am.
K'ódom C'ándi, píwbok'ojtic'oj?am.

To the East, he stretched it out, ac'ój?am.
To the South, he stretched it out, ac'ój?am.
To the West, he stretched it out, ac'ój?am. (50)
To the Northwest, he stretched it out,
ac'ój?am.

K'ódom Beléwdi, píwbok'ojtic'oj?am.

To the North, he stretched it out, ac'ój?am.

Píwbok'ójtibosweten, "Héw!"
ac'ój?am.
"Mí—uním k'awí, uním k'úmpit'i—
c'ewónopem májdym, sól!" ac'ój?am.

When he had stretched it all out, "Good!"
ac'ój?am.
"You—this earth, this mud—
You person who saw it, sing!" ac'ój?am.

"Betéjmemenkydi, k'an,"
—C'iwlutc'onokym
májdym—
"k'ódo jadóm,
k'ódo pulótdom,
ejáwepa?ajk'an, uním k'ódo
sikésdom,
atá mín wónom májdym,
betéjdom,"
ac'ój?am.

"It was in that long ago time, and"
—One Who Throws Over to the Other Side
person—
"creating the world,
sticking the world together,
fixing it long ago, this world
in just such a way,
let mortal people speak of you,
when they tell the ancient stories,"
ac'ój?am. (55)

Amýni sólc'oj?am.
Myk'í k'ódo japéni, ma?át, sóldom,
ek'áwpintic'oj?am.
K'uk'úni
píwbok'ojbosweten,
sóldom, sólwebisim,
c'ájmen sólhekitc'oj?am.

So then he sang, ac'ój?am.
His song, indeed, of world creation,
making it beautiful, ac'ój?am.
When with ropes
they had stretched it all out,
he sang, kept singing,
and by and by he stopped, ac'ój?am.

Amýni k'an, Wépam: "Amá bej, mí bej sól,"
ac'ój?am.
Amýni k'an, sólcoj?am.
Sóldom k'an:

And then to Coyote: "Now, you sing, too,"
ac'ój?am.
And then he sang, ac'ój?am. (60)
Singing thus:

Woodcut by Daniel Stolpe.

"Nik'í kojóm, wat'át'a ynókym k'ódo,
          nik'í," ac'ój?am.
"Wýnnyjnyjc'onodom ynókym k'ódo,
          nik'í," ac'ój?am.
"Jamándatom jamánmantono," ac'ój?am.

"My own valley, world that one may travel
along the edge of, my own," ac'ój?am.
"World that one may travel here and there,
my own," ac'ój?am.
"Mountains piled upon mountains," ac'ój?am.

Awéten k'an, "Nik'í ynókym k'ódo
          kájk'as, sóldom,"
                    ac'ój?am.
"Ka?ápem k'ódojdi k'ás ní ynómapem!"
                    ac'ój?am.

And having done so: "My very own world
where one may travel about!" singing,
ac'ój?am.
"One such as I would travel in a world like
that!" ac'ój?am. (65)

Amýni k'an, K'ódojapem májdym
          sólc'oj?am.
Myk'í japém k'ódo
          sólc'oj?am.
Sólwebisim, sólwebisim, c'ájmen
          sólhekitc'oj?am.

And then, Worldmaker person
sang, ac'ój?am.
He sang of the world that he had made,
ac'ój?am.
He kept singing, kept singing; and by and by
he stopped singing, ac'ój?am.

Awéten, K'ódojapem: "Su,"
          ac'ój?am.
"Uním k'ódo núkti tetébe udóm,
          jahánac'en;
     amá wi?áswajtope?e," ac'ój?am.

Having so done, Worldmaker: "Enough,"
ac'ój?am.
"If this world were a very little bit bigger,
that would be good;
therefore let us stretch it," ac'ój?am. (70)

Ac'ét k'an, Wépam: "Étu!" ac'ój?am.
     "Jahá wéjesí," ac'ój?am.
"Uním k'ódo hésdiwet báljaha,"
                    ac'ój?am.
     "Ek'áwc'etibo adóm," ac'ój?am.
Awéten k'an: "Ai, mínc'om, hesá
ájk'ak'atk'a, mínc'om?" ac'ój?am.

Meanwhile, Coyote: "Wait!" ac'ój?am.
"I speak wisely," ac'ój?am.
"It would be good to paint this world with
something," ac'ój?am.
"So that it will be beautiful to see," ac'ój?am.
Having so spoken: "Hey, you two, what do
you think of that, you two?" ac'ój?am. (75)

Amýni k'an:
C'iwíspolotkym májdym,
          ac'ój?am.
"Ní kak'ás hesí ma?át mákkitmenpem
     majdym," ac'ój?am.

And then it was:
One Who Sticks a Mantle On person,
ac'ój?am.
"I am a person who does not know
anything," ac'ój?am.

Amádi: "Míwet
mínc'om
pénem húk'espem májdyc'om,
uním k'ódo jamádom, húsemwetewdom,
awéten, hesíwet ma?át wasánupe c'edóm,
mínc'om jahátima?amkano," ac'ój?am.
C'íwlutc'onokym
májdym májc'oj?am.

From there: "You two wise persons
to each other,
talking together about it
this world, thinking about it,
then, seeing indeed whatever is bad,
you two will make it good," ac'ój?am.
One Who Throws Over to the Other Side
person said it, ac'ój?am.

Amýni k'an, Wépam májdym: "Héw!"
ac'ój?am.
"Sedéni bálmak'as," ac'ój?am.
"Uním k'ódojdi k'án sedém umápem,"
ac'ój?am.
"Amádi ka?án sedékypem májdym
púkmapem," ac'ój?am.
"Sedékypem k'útt'yt'ym
púkmapem," ac'ój?am.
"Ypék'animt," ac'ój?am.

And then, Coyote person: "Well!"
ac'ój?am. (80)
"I shall color it with blood," ac'ój?am.
"In this world there will be blood,"
ac'ój?am.
"And blood-having people
will be born," ac'ój?am.
"Blood-having birds
will be born," ac'ój?am.
"All kinds," ac'ój?am. (85)

"Symím," ac'ój?am.
"C'ájc'ajnom," ac'ój?am,
"C'ájc'ajnom májdym," ac'ój?am.
"Hesí ma?át, wonómenwet, ypék'anim,
sedékypem, púktamak'an uním k'ódojdi,"
ac'ój?am.
Amýni k'an: "C'ájim k'ódojdi,
láklakpem ka?ánudom,
láklakpem ómudóm umápem," ac'ój?am.

"Deer," ac'ój?am.
"All kinds," ac'ój?am.
"All kinds of people," ac'ój?am.
"Indeed not missing anything, every kind,
having blood, will be born in this world,"
ac'ój?am.
And then: "In various places,
being red,
red rocks will come into being," ac'ój?am. (90)

"Mym mamák'an uním k'ódojdi, sedéni,
ohejtiwonodi, myjákkadom,"
ac'ój?am.
"Adom k'ódom jahatc'etimak'an,"
ac'ój?am.
Wépam májdym májc'oj?am.
"Aj! Mí hesápe húhejjek'a?" ac'ój?am.

"So it shall be that within this world, blood,
mixed up in it, will be the same with them,"
ac'ój?am.
"Then the world will appear beautiful,"
ac'ój?am.
Coyote person said it, mác'ój?am.
"Ay! What do you think of that?" ac'ój?am.

"Mínk'i wéjem jahák'an," ac'ój?am.
"Ní hesí mak'makitmenkas," ac'ój?am.

"Your words are good," ac'ój?am. (95)
"I do not know anything," ac'ój?am.

Woodcut by Daniel Stolpe.

Awéten C'iwíspolotkym
májdym ojk'oj'c'ój?am.
Myk'íonó'yeko:
"Ní kak'ás ejádom píkno ynópem májdym
mamápem,"
ac'ét kájdojdom kájk'ojc'oj?am.

Thereupon, One Who Sticks a Mantle On
person went away, ac'ój?am.
And as he left:
"I shall be a person who only travels in this
way,"
and up and away he flew, ac'ój?am.

K'ódojapem wéjec'oj?am.
"Hénte unínak wusútkinup,"
ac'ój?am.

Worldmaker continued speaking, ac'ój?am.
"Please lie down here on your belly,"
ac'ój?am. (100)

Amýni, "Héw," ac'ój?am.
Awéten jok'óskitdom, wusútkinuc'oj?am.
K'ódo
t'ehýpc'oj?am.
T'ehýhypk'ojdom,
sýttibe t'ehýpk'ojc'oj?am.

So then, "Well," ac'ój?am.
Thereupon he lay on his belly, ac'ój?am.
He stretched out the land
with his feet, ac'ój?am.
He stretched it out with his feet, gradually
he stretched it out with his feet, ac'ój?am.

Ékdadojkydi ik'ún t'ehýhypk'ojc'oj?am.
Awéten, komódi,
awéten Pok'ók'i kýc'onokydi,
t'ehýhypk'ojc'oj?am.
Awéten K'ódom C'ándi
t'ehýhypk'ojc'oj?am.
Awéten K'ódom Beléwdi
t'ehýhypk'ojc'oj?am.

He stretched it out to the East, ac'ój?am. (105)
Then to the South,
then to the West, he pushed it out gradually
with his feet, ac'ój?am.
Then to the Northwest, he pushed it out
gradually with his feet, ac'ój?am.
Then to the North he pushed it out
gradually with his feet, ac'ój?am.

Hadámeni,
hedén t'e?áswajtoweten,
"Su," ac'ój?am.
Amýni k'an, c'ehéwodojc'oj?am.
"Héw! Uním k'ódom áj sy?ýj ynójenak
wémt'ikdykbedom, jahánac'en," ac'ój?am.

Not very far,
having pushed it out just a little way,
"Enough," ac'ój?am.
And so then, he looked up, ac'ój?am. (110)
"Well! It would be good if this world were
big enough to travel around in," ac'ój?am.

Amýni k'an, c'ájmen:
"Hénte béjbym jok'óskitdom, k'ámnak
wusútkinuwet,
c'ehéjhejdojmenmap; wíjjepada!" ac'ój?am.

And so then, by and by:
"Please lie down again, and when you have
stretched out on your belly,
don't look up; don't do it!" ac'ój?am.

Woodcut by Daniel Stolpe.

Amýni k'an, "Héw!" ac'ój?am.
"C'ehéjhejdojmenmak'así," ac'ój?am.
Jok'óskitc'oj?am.

And so then, "Well!" ac'ój?am.
"I won't look up," ac'ój?am.
He lay down on his belly, ac'ój?am. (115)

Ékdadojkydi,
t'ehýhypk'ojdom,
t'edátdiknoc'oj?am.

To the East,
stretching the land out gradually,
he pushed it with his foot as far as he could,
ac'ój?am.

Komónantedi, t'ehýhypsitodom,
t'edátdiknoc'oj?am.

To the South, stretching it around gradually,
he pushed it with his foot as far as he could,
ac'ój?am.

Pok'ókitc'onokynantedi, t'ehýhypsitodom,
t'edátdiknoc'oj?am.

To the West, stretching it around gradually,
he pushed it with his foot as far as he could,
ac'ój?am. (120)

K'ódom C'ánnantedi,
t'ehýhypsitodom,
t'edátdiknoc'oj?am.

To the Northwest, stretching it around
gradually,
he pushed it with his foot as far as he could,
ac'ój?am.

K'ódom Beléwnantedi, t'ehýhypsitodom,
t'edátdiknoc'oj?am.

To the North, stretching it around gradually,
he pushed it with his foot as far as he could,
ac'ój?am.

Awéten, "Su!" ac'ój?am.
Amýni k'an, sywéjkadojc'oj?am.
Sywéjkadojweten,
unínantedi ben?ýnpinc'oj?am.

Having done so, "Enough!" ac'ój?am.
And so then he jumped up, ac'ój?am.
He stepped along hither,
to somewhere around here, ac'ój?am.

Amýni k'an bej,
my?úsim týswonojec'oj?am.
Ámkanim ynódojdom, ynódojdom,
Komónantedi ynóc'oj?am.
Ýnnodom, yk'ójc'oj?am.
Ántedi, Pok'ók'ihínk'ojkynantedi amám kikí
ysítodom,
K'ódom C'ándi jysítodi yc'ónodom,

And so then again,
this one was standing there alone, ac'ój?am.
Finally going up, going up,
he went Southward, ac'ój?am.
Going along, he departed, ac'ój?am. (125)
Afterwards, to the West,
kept going across and around
to the Northwest, traveling from there

K'ódom Beléwdi, ypék'ano hac'ónodom,

Ékdadojkydi yc'ónoweten k'an

myk'í wýnnynyjdojwonopem k'ódojdi
ydíknoweten k'an, sikésc'oj?am.

Péne pének'an, jac'ój?am —
edáldalnopem májdym.
Awéten, béjbym dáldalnowet núktı
c'ájtikkapem, jac'ój?am.
Hem'makdom, jac'ój?am

Jawébisim, sýtti síwsiwpe jac'ój?am.
Awéten, sýtti núkti síwsiwhudojpe
jac'ój?am.
Pénene píkno jac'ójam.

Awéten, k'ódo
hémmakc'oj?am.
Hémmakkebisim, k'ódo méjc'oj?am.

"Uním jákypem k'ódom
uním májdy kymá?amkano";
ejáwinim májdym: "mí, jakýtidom,
k'ódo kymák'an," ac'ój?am.

Awéten: "Uním májdym k'an
díwebisim, díwebisim,
pínini k'úmmenc'ikdom, pínini ékdadom,
díwebisim, díwebisim,
myk'í k'úmmenim wosípdom, myk'í ékdam
wosípmyni kak'án,
uním májdym, díbospem, púkmapem,"
ac'ój?am.
"Tetét pínini k'úmmenim wosípdom,
púkmak'an," ac'ój?am.

to the North, traveling from one place to
another,
to the East, he was going, and
he came to a place he had departed from
long before,
he arrived there,
and he stopped and got things ready, ac'ój?am.

He made them, two by two, ac'ój?am —
White people.
Having done this, he made another white pair,
but a little different, ac'ój?am.
Counting, he made them, ac'ój?am. (130)

He kept on, and made a black pair, ac'ój?am.
Having done so, he made another black pair,
which were a little different, ac'ój?am.
He made them only in pairs, ac'ój?am.

This done, he counted off all the lands,
ac'ój?am.
Counting and counting, he gave land to
them, ac'ój?am. (135)

"This name-having place
shall have this people";
to each sort of people: "you, naming places,
shall have a country," ac'ój?am.

With this established: "These people
will keep growing, keep growing,
many winters come, many mornings dawn,
keep growing, keep growing,
their winters passing, their mornings
passing until
this people, fully grown, shall be born,"
ac'ój?am.
"Very many winters passing,
they will be born," ac'ój?am.

Woodcut by Daniel Stolpe.

Amám, kak'án: Thereupon:
"tét'yt'ykydom   "they will be children-having people,
pókydom, p'ýbekydom,   daughter-having, son-having,
apém tét'ytym, díbosdom,   so the children, being fully grown,
tét'yt'ykydom mamák'an,"   shall be people who again have children,"
ac'ój?am.   ac'ój?am.
Amýni kak'án: So then:
"hesánbem k'úmmenim wosípc'et,   "when many winters have gone by,
teteł pím májdym mamápem," ac'ój?am.   there will be very many people," ac'ój?am. (140)

Awéten, béjbym,   Having done so, again,
c'ájtikwinim májdy, béjbym,   to other kinds of people, again,
sýttim k'ódo, béjbym, méjc'oj?am.   he gave, again, a country, ac'ój?am.

Adóm k'an wéjec'oj?am.   And then he kept speaking, ac'ój?am.
Uním májdym, k'an: To this people:
"ka?ás mínsy uním k'ódojdi sówonodom,"   "henceforth to you I am leaving this
ac'ój?am.   country," ac'ój?am.
"Amám k'an, ka?ámkano uním k'ódo   "And so, you shall have this country,"
kymápem," ac'ój?am.   ac'ój?am.
"Jakýpem májdym mamá?amkano,"   "You shall be people who have names,"
ac'ój?am.   ac'ój?am. (145)

"Myk'ím k'an, béjby,   "All of them, also,
c'ájtikwinim májdym,   different kinds of people,
jakýpem májdym béjby   will be people who also have names
myk'í k'ódom ka?án béjby jakýpem,"   and their places will also have names,"
ac'ój?am.   ac'ój?am.
"Mínk'i k'ódom, béjby, jakýpem k'ódom   "Your country, also, will be a country that
mamák'an," ac'ój?am.   has names," ac'ój?am.
"Mí béjby jakýma?amkano," ac'ój?am.   "You also will have names," ac'ój?am.
"Amám ka?ámkano uním k'ódojdi,   "Henceforth you will be in this world
k'an mínk'i tét'yt'ym opítmak'an," ac'ój?am.   and your children will fill it up," ac'ój?am.
"Lútpek'anim tét'yt'ym   "Each and every one of the children you
kak'án   have will be
jakýpem mamápem," ac'ój?am.   people who have names," ac'ój?am. (150)

"Amádi, díwebisim,   "There, keep growing,
pím k'úmmenim wosípdom,   many winters passing,

Woodcut by Daniel Stolpe.

pím ekím wosípdom,
díbosmaʔamkano," ac'ójʔam.
"Adóm kaʔámkano unim k'ódo kymápem,"
ac'ójʔam.

many dawns passing,
you shall be fully grown," ac'ójʔam.
"Henceforth this land will be yours,"
ac'ójʔam.

Awéten, sýttibe wéjec'ojʔam.

Having done this, he spoke once more,
ac'ójʔam.

Béjbym, c'ájtikkawinim majdy, béjby
k'ódo méjc'ojʔam.

Also, to a different sort of person, also,
he gave land, ac'ójʔam.

Wéjec'ojʔam.
"Mí mamáʔamkano c'ájtikkat wéjepem
májdym,
c'ájtikc'etípem májdym," ac'ójʔam.
"Amám, kaʔámkano, mí béjby k'ódojkypem
mamáʔamkano," ac'ójʔam.
"Mínk'i tét'yt'ym, wokódom, kaʔán uním
kódojnan,
c'áj jákypem k'ódo,
k'ódojdi bísjahadom,
yk'ójdom bísmapem,"
ac'ójʔam.
"Amádi, ypék'anim, k'ódojdi opítmak'an,
púkkinudom," ac'ójʔam.

He spoke, ac'ójʔam. (155)
"You shall be people who speak
differently,
people who appear differently," ac'ójʔam.
Then, "you, in turn, shall have
a country, you shall have it," ac'ójʔam.
"Your children, weary, will go from this
place,
to a place with a different name,
a place where it is good to live,
they will go away and remain there,"
ac'ójʔam.
"And so, being born, they will live on every
bit of the world," ac'ójʔam.

Adóm k'an, k'ódo c'etócojʔam.

And so he divided the lands among them,
ac'ójʔam. (160)

C'ájtikkape myná méjje, béjby,
sýtti mym k'ódojna mejje:
"Ypék'anim májdym mí kaʔámkano
c'áji jakýpem mamápem,"
adóm k'an mejje
ac'ójʔam.

To one giving one sort, and in turn,
to another giving a different place:
"All of you people shall
have different names,"
and so he gave something to them all,
ac'ójʔam.

Awéten k'an, c'ájmen,
ynódojdom, ypínc'ojʔam.
Yjéwebisim, yjéwebisim,
K'ódo Éstodi okítweten,

And having done so, by and by,
going on, he came back this way, ac'ójʔam.
He kept going, kept going,
having arrived at the Middle of the World,

k'an, sikésc'oj?am.
Péne jawéten, utíc'oj?am.

and then, he prepared it, ac'új?am.
Having made two, he left them there,
ac'új?am.

"Uním ka?amkano díwebisim,
hesánbem k'úmmenim, ma?át, wosípc'et,
tetét pím k'úmmenim, pím ekím
wosípc'et,
ka?ámkano díbosmapem," ac'új?am.
"Adóm, ka?ámkano wónom májdym,
mamápem díbospem, púkmapem,"
ac'új?am.

"You will keep growing here,
how many winters, indeed, having gone by,
very many winters, many dawns
having gone by,
you shall fully grow," ac'új?am. (165)
"And so, you will be mortal people,
you shall fully grow, you shall be born,"
ac'új?am.

"Uním k'ódom ka?án jakýpem mamápem,"
ac'új?am.
"Uním jamánim, kíwdi c'ájim k'ódo;
mym béjby jakýpem mamák'an,"
ac'új?am.

"This country shall have a name,"
ac'új?am.
"This mountain, behind it is another country;
that shall also be one that has a name,"
ac'új?am.

Amám: "Béjdykmeni,
k'an, ka?ámkano,
púkmapem," ac'új?am.

Thereupon: "It is not yet your turn,
but, sufficiently grown
you shall have a birth," ac'új?am.

Unídi, K'ódom Éstodi,
sówonoweten,
yk'ójc'oj?am.

Here, from the Middle Of The World,
having departed,
he went off, ac'új?am. (170)

Yk'ójjebisim,
wémt'ik'im k'ódona yk'újdom,
wónom májdyk'i bísmape,
wojí ydíknoweten,
k'an jesánoc'oj?am.
Awetén k'an, mydí béj sikésc'oj?am.

He kept going away,
going off to just those places
where mortal people were to live,
having reached that far,
and he stopped, ac'új?am.
Having so done, he again prepared things,
ac'új?am.

Péne, ac'új?am.
Béjbym péne, ac'új?am,
Wokítc'oj?am.

Two, ac'új?am.
Again two, ac'új?am,
He put down, ac'új?am. (175)

Woodcut by Daniel Stolpe.

Béjbym péne, ac'ój?am,
Wokítc'oj?am.

Again two, ac'ój?am,
He put down, ac'ój?am.

Hémmakkebisim, hémmakbosweten, k'an
wéjec'oj?am.
"Mí unídi bísma?amkano," ac'ój?am.
"Mínk'i k'ódok'an
jakýpem mamá?amkano," ac'ój?am.
"Núktim tetémenim k'ódojdi, ma?át
bíswet,
wémt'ikma?amkano," ac'ój?am.

Counting them out, counted them all out, and
he spoke, ac'ój?am.
"You shall remain here," ac'ój?am.
"You and your country
will be ones who have names," ac'ój?am. (180)
"Staying in a country that is little, indeed not
big,
it will be enough for you," ac'ój?am.

Uním: "Sówonowonos,
amám díwebisim, díwebisim,
hesánbem k'úmmenim wosípdom,
tetét pím k'úmmenim wosípdom,
tetét pím ekím wosípdom,
díbosma?amkano," ac'ój?am.

This: "Once I have left,
you will keep growing, keep growing,
how many winters passing,
a great many winters passing,
a great many days passing,
you will have grown enough," ac'ój?am.

"Adóm, ka?ámkano díbospem,
púkmapem," ac'ój?am.
"Anímmyni, mínk'i pekým,
c'ájc'ajnom pekým,
homóbokitmenim pekým dímak'an;
amýni, ka?ámkano
wémt'ik'i húkespem púkdom,
hónwenumapem," ac'ój?am.

"Then, when you have grown enough,
you shall be born," ac'ój?am.
"At that time, your food,
different kinds of food,
any kind of food, shall grow;
and you, having been
born with enough intelligence,
shall survive," ac'ój?am.

Awéten,
k'adótkitc'oj?am.

Having so done,
he shoved them under the ground,
ac'ój?am. (185)

Awetén, béjby wéjec'oj?am.

Having so done, he spoke again, it's said.

"Mí, béjby, béjby núktim k'ódokypem
mamá?amkano," ac'ój?am.
'Héw! Uním k'ódojnan c'ájnap!'
adóm batásipdom c'ájim kojóna,
batác'ono totomenkym májdym
mamá?amkano.

"You, in turn, will also be ones who have a
small country," ac'ój?am.
"'Hey! Clear out of this country!'
thereby driving others from their valleys,
you shall not become this kind of people."

Woodcut by Daniel Stolpe.

"Mí, mamáʔamkano,
c'ájtikkat jawímapem mínk'i k'ódo,"
ac'ójʔam.
"Mí béjby c'ájtikkape jakýpem májdym,
mamáʔamkano," ac'ójʔam.

"Amám, kaʔámkano díwebisim, díwebisim,
pím ekím wosípnodom,
pím k'úmmenim wosípmyni,
púkmapem,
mínk'i púkmapem ekím
wosípomyni," ac'ójʔam.

"Amám kaʔámkano tét'yt'y kydóm, béjbym,
c'ájim k'úmmeni wosípc'et,
tetébe yjédom,
awébisim k'an, díwebisim,
k'úmmenc'ikbosdom bej,
béwkinuwebisim,
wémt'ik'im májdym mamáʔamkano,"
ac'ójʔam.

"Mínk'i tét'yt'ym,
sýttim maʔát wonómenwet,
ypék'anim kaʔán jakýpem mamápem,"
ac'ójʔam.
"Uním k'ódom, béjby, myjákkapem,
k'an jakýpem," ac'ójʔam.

"Ypék'anim k'ódom jakýpem mamák'an;
mí jákkapem amának:
ka'ámkano c'enók'ojdom,
amýni, yk'ójmadom:
'mym k'ódojna ynómak'as,'
adóm jawímapem manímmyni,
kak'án ypék'anim májdym mákkitmapem
mínk'i yk'ójpe," ac'ójʔam.

"You, becoming,
will have other names for your countries,"
ac'ójʔam.
"You will also have other names for people,
as you become," ac'ójʔam.

"Thereupon, keep growing, keep growing,
many dawns passing,
many winters having passed,
you shall be born,
when the dawn of your own birth has
passed," ac'ójʔam. (190)

"Thereupon you will have children, in turn,
other winters go by,
they will get a little bigger,
and going on like that, keep growing,
after enough winters have passed again,
they will keep growing,
there will be enough people,"
ac'ójʔam.

"Your children,
indeed not missing even one,
will all have names,"
ac'ójʔam.
"This country, also, it will be the same with it,
having names," ac'ójʔam.

"Every place will have a name;
you can call it by name:
you will be going some other place,
so then, as you go:
'I'm going to that country,'
so when you call it by name,
then every person will know
where you are going," ac'ójʔam.

Awéten k'an, unínantedi,
hémmakdom,
sówonoc'oj?am.
Awéten k'an, unínantedi: "mí béjby,"
ac'új?am.
"Béjby, wónom májdym mamá?amkano
hesánbeniniwet k'úmmenim
wosípc'onodom,
pím k'úmmenim wosípk'ojpedi,
ka?ámkano púkmapem," ac'új?am.

"Díwebisim," ac'új?am.
"K'úmmen núkti,
tetét tibí díma?amkano," ac'új?am.
"Béjbym, k'úmmenim wosípmyni,
díwebisim,
pím k'úmmenim yc'ónomyni,
díbosma?amkano," ac'új?am.

"Adóm k'an, ka?ámkano, díbospem,
púkmapem," ac'új?am.

"Amádi, mí béjby k'ódo kymá?amkano,"
ac'új?am.
"Mínk'i k'ódom ka'án jakýpem mamápem;
mí béjby jakýpem mamá?amkano,"
ac'új?am.

"Amám,
májdym tét'yt'y kymádom ka?ámkano,
mínk'i tét'yt'ym, tetébet'yt'ýmyni,
uním k'ódo c'ehéjhejk'ojdom;
japájtodom,
amýni k'ódo mákpajdom;
amýni k'ódo jawídom;
adóm mákpapajtidom tét'yt'y mínk'i
jawímapem," ac'új?am.

And having done so, on this side,
counting out the people,
he left them, ac'új?am. (195)
Having done so, on this side: "you also,"
ac'új?am.
"You, too, shall become mortal people,
how many winters
passing,
many winters having passed on this side,
you shall be born," ac'új?am.

"Keep growing," ac'új?am.
"Each winter,
you will get a little bigger," ac'új?am.
"Again, winters having passed,
keep growing,
many winters having passed,
you will be fully ready," ac'új?am.

"Then, when you are ready, completely ready,
you shall be born," ac'új?am. (200)

"There, you will also have a country,"
ac'új?am.
"Your country will be one that has a name;
you too will be one who has a name,"
ac'új?am.

"Thereupon,
being people who have children,
your children having gotten a little bigger,
will look about around this country;
speaking well,
so teaching them about the land;
so naming the country for them;
then you will teach your children
to know names," ac'új?am.

Woodcut by Daniel Stolpe.

"'Myjákkapem k'ódom ka?án,
myjákkapem jamánim ka?án mým'
adóm, ka?ámkano mákpapajtinimmyni,
mí jákk'at mákkitmapem,"
ac'ój?am.
Awéten k'an, dyký́ty?ysitoc'oj ?am.

Adóm k'an, myk'í hémmakjo
méjbosmadom,
sýtti awónomc'oj?am.

"Mí béjby," ac'ój?am,
"Mí ma?ámkano c'ájt'ikk'at wéjepem
májdym;
núkti pítom mamá?amkano," ac'ój?am.
"Mí, béjby, myjákkapem,"
ac'ój?am.
"Uním ka'an ma?ándykbem k'ódom
ka?án tetém k'ódom," ac'ój?am.
"Amádi nik'í ynówonosmyni,
ka?án hesí ma?át wi?ímenmapem," ac'ój?am.

K'òdo héwwakaktomotoc'oj?am.

"Nik'í ásmam
k'ódom wi?ímenmapem umák'an,"
ac'ój?am.
"Amádi: mín wewéjbosdom:
'mín kaníwonom bíshukitmadom,' kájk'as,"
ac'ój?am.
"Mí ka?ámkano kaním májdym,"
ac'ój?am.
"Amádi mín bíshukitweten,
jewéjdom bísmak'as,"
ac'ój?am.
"Amám uním k'ódo jahámenmyni,
jadý́kdykmak'as;

"'This place has a name,
that mountain has a name,'
then, you shall be teaching them,
teaching them to know what you know,"
ac'ój?am. (205)
Having done so, he snapped them away,
ac'ój?am.

And then, as he was about to finish counting
them all,
one still remained, ac'ój?am.

"You, also," ac'ój?am.
"You will be people who speak
differently;
there will be a little too many of you," ac'ój?am.
"For you, in turn, like the others,"
ac'ój?am. (210)
"It will be a large country,
it will be a big country," ac'ój?am.
"Wherever I have traveled,
you will indeed want for nothing," ac'ój?am.

He motioned to the world in all directions,
ac'ój ?am.

"Wherever I have been
the world shall continue to lack for nothing,"
ac'ój?am.
There: "completing my speech for you:
'may you dwell here all your life,' I say,"
ac'ój?am.
"You shall be the last of my people,"
ac'ój?am. (215)
"Now that I have told you to dwell here,
I shall depart and remain over there,"
ac'ój?am.
"If things are not just right in this country,
I shall make them so;

Woodcut by Daniel Stolpe.

amám jadýkdykʔis,
amám, héki, púkmaʔamkano," ac'ójʔam.

and when I have done that,
then, later, you will be born," ac'ójʔam.

Wépam májdym, hésmen,
húpajc'ojʔam.
Adóm, májc'ojʔam.
"Amádi, uním k'ódom kaʔán
t'ijýkmapem," ac'ójʔam.
"Uním k'ódo, ypé bánhyt'anudom,
kak'án k'ódom hetílkitmenwet," ac'ójʔam.

Coyote person, long before,
divined all this, ac'ójʔam.
Then he said, mác'ójʔam: (220)
"Henceforth, this world shall
have tremors," ac'ójʔam.
"This world, being all flat and thin,
it shall not be stable," ac'ójʔam.

"Amádi, uním k'ódo
jabósweten,
c'ájmen, ebýdom,
uním k'uk'ú wikúkumak'así," ac'ójʔam.
"Ásmyni, uním k'ódom hetílkitmak'an,"
ac'ójʔam.
"Nik'í k'uk'ú, kaʔás wikúkudom,
t'ijýktimapem," ac'ójʔam.

"Therefore, this world having been
completely fixed,
by and by, from time to time,
I shall tug on this rope," ac'ójʔam.
"Afterwards, this world shall stablize,"
ac'ójʔam.
"My rope, I shall tug now and then,
I am the one that shall cause it to tremble,"
ac'ójʔam. (225)

Awéten, "Sú!" ac'ójʔam,
"Solím umák'an," ac'ójʔam.
"Wiʔímenmak'an," ac'ójʔam.
"Jymáʔamkano mínsym," ac'ójʔam.

Having so done, "Enough!" ac'ójʔam.
"There will be songs," ac'ójʔam.
"They shall not be lacking," ac'ójʔam.
"All of you will have them," ac'ójʔam.

Aweten, sólc'ojʔam.
Sóllebisim, sóllebisim,
sólhekitc'ojʔam.

Having so done, he sang, ac'ójʔam. (230)
Kept singing, kept singing,
then he stopped singing, ac'ójʔam.

Awéten, "uním solí
mínsym wónom májdym kymáʔamkano,"
ac'ójʔam.

Having so done, "these are the songs that
you mortal people will have,"
ac'ójʔam.

Awéten, bej,
c'áji sólc'ojʔam.
Awéten, c'áji sóldom,
yjéc'ojʔam.

Having so done, again,
he sang some other songs, ac'ójʔam.
Thereupon, singing some other songs,
he started off, ac'ójʔam.

Woodcut by Daniel Stolpe.

Yjéwebisim,
K'ódom Éstodi okítkanim,

ynódom mydí obýʔasʔino,
bydójdom, bísc'ojʔam.

He kept going,
until he finally came to the Middle of the
World,
when he got that far,
he sat down, he stayed there, ac'ójʔam. (235)

Amét, k'ódo jántodom,
C'iwísp'olotkym májdym
ek'áwpintipe sólc'ojʔam.
Mým mac'ójʔam,
Jahójjapem májdym,
pówoc'onom kojókypem májdym
mac'ójʔam.

Thus, creating the world,
Robin person
sang very beautifully, ac'ójʔam.
He, ac'ójʔam,
He was the first person made,
the first person to go across the valley,
ac'ójʔam.

K'awí c'epém májdym
tetét ek'áwpintidom solí
betéjtom solí
Sólpem májdym

Earth-seeing person
very beautiful songs
ancient songs
Song-singing person

Amádi k'an, K'ódojapem, ynódom,
K'ódom Éstodi ywálawweten,
hybó hakítdom,
bísc'ojʔam.

And there, Worldmaker, traveling,
went past the Middle of the World,
built a house,
and stayed there, ac'ójʔam. (240)

Kaní wój ydíknoc'ojʔam.
Kaním, ac'ójʔam.

He was there at the ends of the earth, ac'ójʔam.
That is all, ac'ójʔam.

FIVE

Hompajtotokymc'om / The Adversaries

Hómpajtotokyc'om	The Adversaries
"K'ódo helájtapyʔy," ac'ójʔam.	"Let us two gamble for the world," ac'ójʔam.

Amám k'an, ékdabosmadom,	Thereupon, just about dawn,
kaním bénekto k'an, pelípwek'ojc'ojʔam.	and on the last morning, he called out, ac'ójʔam.
K'ódom ékdajedom, jodádalc'opinc'et,	As the sun rose, just it was becoming light,
pelípwek'ojc'ojʔam.	he called out, ac'ójʔam.
Béjbym pedátowek'ojc'ojʔam.	Again, they called back to him, ac'ójʔam.
Ypékanbem k'ódojnan	From every part of the land,
pelípwek' ojc'ojʔam.	they called out, ac'ójʔam.

Unínante,	It was not so far from here,
pok'ók'i hínk'ojkym,	just yonder,
k'anájwositodi,	across from where the sun floats down,
betéjmen, betejtodi,	that long ago, in olden times,
betéjim ynódojc'ójʔam.	an ancient being was going along, ac'ójʔam.

Unínan:	From hereabouts:
"k'ódo helájtapyʔy," ac'ójʔam.	"let us two gamble for the world," ac'ójʔam.
"Ní, uním k'ódojdi, Wépam májdym,	"I, in this world, Coyote person,
uním k'ódo ynódom,	going along in this world,
uním k'ódo wíhjamak'as!" ac'ójʔam.	I will ruin this world!" ac'ójʔam.

Amýni, "Héw héw" ac'ójʔam,	Then, "Well, well!" ac'ójʔam.
"Kaʔápe wejédom,	"If you talk like that,
uním k'ódojdi wiʔímaʔamkano!"	you'll not be in this world for long!"
ac'ójʔam.	ac'ójʔam. (5)

Amýni k'an, mymý kaʔájmyni,	And then, when the one had spoken thus,
ynódojc'ojʔam.	the other set out, ac'ójʔam.
Ynódojdom k'an, yk'ójc'ojʔam.	He went on and went away, ac'ójʔam.

Lithograph by Daniel Stolpe.

Ac'ét k'an, byjí wéjec'oj?am.

And meanwhile, the people declared a feast, ac'ój?am.

Jepónim k'an hýhwejc'oj?am.
Hýhwejjebisim, myk'í májdy wéjedom,
       wéjec'oj?am.

And their leader said great things, ac'ój?am.
He talked and talked to his people,
ac'ój?am. (10)

Amýni, sýttim jepónim p'únc'oj?am.

Then one leader was knotting strings,
ac'ój?am.

P'únnebisim, betéjtodi,
hesánbem k'ódojdiwet,
májdyk'i bíspem k'ódojdi,
    p'únnemadom
      p'únc'oj?am.
Májdyk'i bískym t'íkk'ojdi,
    hémmamaknoc'oj?am.
Walási hémmakdom p'únc'oj?am.
Awébisim tawálbosc'oj?am.
    Awéten: "Sú," ac'ój?am.

Knotting many strings, in an ancient time,
for as many kinds in that long-ago country,
for as many places where people lived,
he knotted strings
in order to send them out, ac'ój?am.
The various places where people lived,
he counted them, ac'ój?am.
He counted out the knotted strings, ac'ój?am.
By and by the task was done, ac'ój?am. (15)
And then: "Enough," ac'ój?am.

"Mí ynóp, mym k'ódojdi," ac'oj?am.
"Kok'ók'i Kýnc'onokydi ynóp," ac'oj?am.
"K'ódom C'ándi ynóp," ac'oj?am.
"Májdyk'i bískym t'ik'ójdi ynóp," ac'oj?am.

"You there, go to that country," ac'ój?am.
"You go to the West," ac'ój?am.
"And you other go to the Northwest," ac'ój?am.
"Go to where people live," ac'ój?am.

"Mí uním K'ódom Beléwdi ysítop," ac'oj?am.
"Májdyk'i bískym t'ik'ójdi ynóp," ac'oj?am.

"And you go along to the North." ac'ój?am.
"Go to where people live," ac'ój?am. (20)

"Mí uním Ékdadojkydi ynóp." ac'oj?am.
"Uním Pok'ók'i Hínk'omónantedi:
uním ekím pok'óm hiná yt'ákym,
k'anájwositodi ynópi," ac'oj?am.
    "Wónom májdyk'i bískym
      k'ódo yt'ájmenwet,
      ynópada," ac'oj?am.

"You, go this way toward the East," ac'ój?am.
"You, go this way to the South:
where the sun turns to go down,
where it goes straight over," ac'ój?am.
"Where mortal people live,
overlooking no place
go there," ac'ój?am. (25)

Adóm, jepónim wéjec'oj?am.
    "C'ebó nik'í," ac'oj?am.
    "Japájtotok'así," ac'oj?am.

So the leader spoke, ac'ój?am.
"Let them come see me," ac'ój?am.
"I would talk with them," ac'ój?am.

Lithograph by Daniel Stolpe.

Amýni yk'ójc'oj?am.
Yk'ójpem, c'ájmen okíkittojec'oj?am.

Then they set off, ac'ój?am.
And going, after a time they returned,
ac'ój?am. (30)

Amám helunini ékdawosipc'et,
myjím k'ódojnak,
ypék'andykbem k'ódojnan okítc'oj?am.
Okíttebisim, okíttebisim,
okítbosc'oj?am.

When only a few days had passed,
from all lands,
people came to that place, ac'ój?am.
They kept arriving, kept arriving,
until all had arrived, ac'ój?am.

Okítbosweten,
jepónim májdym hýhwejc'oj?am.

When they were all arrived,
their leader addressed them, ac'ój?am.

"Héw" ac'ój?am.
"'Jahám k'ódo wéjek'as,'" ac'ój?am.
"'Uním k'ódom jahábo,' ak'ási," ac'ój'am.
"Ásmyni, 'Wíjjek'an, hesádom uním
wónokym
k'útt'yt'ym mapém,
mykán puk'úkinu mak'áde?'
ak'án nik'í," ac'ój?am.
"'Wónokym k'útt'yt'ym ka?án wónodom,
wónomapem,' ak'án nik'í,"
ac'ój?am.
"'Hesádom mak'á wónopem, béj,
ynójemapem?
ka?ámenmapem ka?áno,'
ak'án nik'í," ac'ój?am.

"Well!" ac'ój?am.
"'Let this be a good world,'" ac'ój?am.
"'Let this world be good,' I say," ac'ój?am. (35)
"But 'No, why should these kinds of
mortal beings,
having died,
come back to life again?'
so he said to me," ac'ój?am.
"'When mortal beings die,
they should stay dead,' so he said to me,"
ac'ój?am.
"'Why should a dead man, again,
come to be walking around?
you are just not going to arrange it that way,'
so he said to me," ac'ój?am.

"'Ní ka?ás hésmenim májdym betéjmen k'an
betéjmemenkydi wónodom, wónot'a,'
apa?ájk'an,
'amám, ypédi ka?ámkano wónopem,
tújc'enodom,
sywéjwejdojweten,
týswonojemenmapem;
mým ka?án wónokym k'ódo jawónopem,'"
ac'ój?am.
"'Mymým as wónoc'ojk'an, amám k'an,

"'I am the first person of olden times and
I say let the old ones die when they die,' he
said,
"'afterwards, when they're dead,
waking up,
getting to their feet and standing there,
they're not going to do this;
they shall know a world with death in it,'"
ac'ój?am. (40)
"'If they die, and then afterwards,

Lithograph by Daniel Stolpe.

mykánim hónwejdom kak'án,
ynójedom,
aménmapem kak'án,
homónim maʔáti,'" ac'ójʔam.

they were to be breathing,
they would be going about,
it should not be this way,
indeed no matter who they are!'" ac'ójʔam.

"Ak'án nik'í," ac'ójʔam.

"So he said to me," ac'ójʔam.

"Amám: 'Uním k'ódo
ysítojedom,
uním k'ódo c'ebýkmak'as,'
ak'án nik'í," ac'ójʔam.

"After that: 'In this world
I'm going to wander around;
I will take a good look at this world,'
so he said to me," ac'ójʔam.

Amýni: "Wasók'as," ac'ójʔam.

Then: "I am angry," ac'ójʔam.

"Nik'í májdym, mínsym
uním k'ódom jýmotodi,
uním momím,
mómboc'onopem bat'át'as
jýmotodi;
ókk'etwonom maʔámkano mínsym,"
ac'ójʔam.

"My own people, you must all search about
this land,
these waters,
to the very edge where the water flows
about it;
you must be vigilant,"
ac'ójʔam. (45)

"Ypék'andykbem k'ódojdi,
mínsym Wépa wónotipada," ac'ójʔam.
"Tetét jahámenk'an; wasák'an," ac'ójʔam.
"Hesí maʔát, ník
t'íkc'emenk'an,"
ac'ójʔam.

"Wherever he might be in the world,
you must kill Coyote," ac'ójʔam.
"He is no good at all; he is bad," ac'ójʔam.
"Indeed, he would
not believe me in anything,"
ac'ójʔam.

"'Mínsyk'i kaʔas,
wónotimenmapem;
amádi, mínsym ník,
jeponim májdy, wasótidom kaʔámkano;
mínsywet
uním k'ódo sikésdom, jahátidom;
k'ódojkymenmapem,'
ak'án nik'í," ac'ójʔam.

"'Left up to you,
there would be no death; [Coyote speaking].
and there, you're making me,
the leader of the people, angry,
you would have it be you alone
arranging this world, making it good;
you shall never have the world,'
he said to me," ac'ójʔam. (50)

"'"Tetém jepóni ónk'ojc'ojk'an,"
adóm ník ypék'andykbem
k'ódom jýwajtokynan wéjekinutodom,
ník núkpapajmenmak'an,'
ak'án nik'í," ac'ój?am.

"Mymým, Wépam majdym, hap
ónk'ojti?usc'yjk'an,
adóm k'an:
'Ník, jepónim májdym ma?át;
hesi ma?át makkitmenpe
jákwejdom;
núkpapajmenma?amkano!'" ac'ój?am.
"Ak'án nik'í," ac'ój?am.
"Awéten, wás?ýk'ojk'an," ac'ój?am.

"Ní jahát wéjek'as," ac'ój?am.
"'Wónom májdym wi?ímenkym matá,'
ak'ási," ac'ój?am.
"'Hesádowet, ma?át, wónoc'et,
mómdi wowóc'onomymi,
bénekto tújc'onokym matá,'
adóm ní wéjek'asi," ac'ój?am.

"Ac'ét onó myk'í o?ý?ylymdom:
'Ka?ámenmapem kak'án;
wasá káj?amkano, wéjedom!
hesádom mak'á wónoweten
bénekto ynójemapem?'
ak'án nik'í," ac'ój?am.

Amám,
"Mínk'i májdy wéjebene?e,"
ac'ój?am.
"Unínan ypínim májdy," ac'ój?am.
"Mí wéjebene?e mínk'i májdy," ac'ój?am.

"Uním pok'ók'i kyc'ónokynantedim májdy,
mí jepónim májdym,
ka?ámkano," ac'ój?am.

"'"He overcame the great leader,"
so that's the news about me
they will say throughout the world,
they'll not laugh at me,'
he said to me," ac'ój?am.

"He, Coyote person, seems
to defeat himself,
like so:
'I am, indeed a leader of the people;
you are not going to say
I don't know anything;
you are not going to laugh at me!'" ac'ój?am.
"So he said to me," ac'ój?am.
"Thereupon he angrily started off," ac'ój?am.

"I spoke well," ac'ój?am.
"'Mortal persons shall not cease to exist,'
I told him," ac'ój?am. (55)
"'From, indeed, whatever cause they die,
let them be stretched out in the water,
in the morning let them awaken,'
thusly I spoke," ac'ój?am.

"But he shook his head:
'That's not the way it's going to be;
what you're saying is bad!
how is it that anyone who has died
could be going around the next morning?'
he said to me," ac'ój?am.

Then,
"You had better go tell that to your people,"
ac'ój?am.
"People come hither," ac'ój?am.
"You go tell that to your people," ac'ój?am. (60)

"People who live in the west,
you who are the leader of that people,
go do this," ac'ój?am.

Lithograph by Daniel Stolpe.

"Mí, unínan ysítopem májdym,
wéjebeneʔe mínkʼi májdy," acʼójʔam.

"You, who went across from the northwest,
go tell your people," acʼójʔam.

Mysém májdy haʔáj wotópajjahakʼan,
acʼójʔam.

You do the same, people from the north,
acʼójʔam.

"Mí uníméekdadojkynan ýnpinpem májdym,
wéjebeneʔe mínkʼi májdy," acʼójʔam.

"You people who come from the east,
go and tell your people," acʼójʔam.

"Ypékʼanim kʼódojdi,
týswokitbeneʔe mínsym," acʼójʔam.

"In each and every country,
you must be alert," acʼójʔam. (65)

Amýni, "Héw!" acʼójʔam.

Then, "Well!" acʼójʔam.

"Wépa wónotidojdom,
wónotiweten,
pínhejetapeʔe," acʼójʔam.
"Cʼýjim ekím, cʼýjim ekím wosípcʼet,
pelílipnomendom,
wónotiboskaʔemkʼes,
atápeʔe," acʼójʔam.

"In killing Coyote,
after having killed him,
you must listen," acʼójʔam.
"Four days, four days having passed,
if you don't hear him howling,
we will have really killed him,
let it be so," acʼójʔam.

"Myméntapo," acʼójʔam,
"Uní Wépakʼi cʼucʼúwono,
pitʼíwono,
ypékʼani mínsym hatámpada,"
acʼójʔam.
"Báwonope kaʔápepe,
mínsym wonónomenpada," acʼójʔam.
"Kʼodomtíkdi mínsym hatámpada," acʼójʔam.

"At the same time," acʼójʔam,
"Every place where Coyote has pissed
where he has shat,
every one of you must go and find them,"
acʼójʔam. (70)
"Where he has scratched the dirt,
don't any of you miss these places," acʼójʔam.
"Search all over this land," acʼójʔam.

Amýni, "Héw," acʼójʔam.

Then, "Well!" acʼójʔam.

Acʼét,
Wépam hokóttitobosim kaním,
ynódojcʼójʔam.
Ykʼójcʼojʔam.

Meanwhile,
when Coyote's dispute had come to an end,
he went off, acʼójʔam.
Going away, acʼójʔam. (75)

Uním kokókʼi kýcʼonokynantedi ynócʼojʔam.
Háscʼojʔam.

He went off to the west, acʼójʔam.
He lifted his leg, acʼójʔam.

Lithograph by Daniel Stolpe.

Dý háspajc'oj?am.

He lifted his leg against the bushes, ac'ój?am.

Bewésc'oj?am.

He scratched the ground with his hind feet,
ac'ój?am.

Sewím k'ýsdi, ma?át,
ymítc'oj?am.

A sandbar in the river, indeed,
he got onto it, ac'ój?am. (80)

Mydí bewésc'oj?am.

There he scratched with his hind feet,
ac'ój?am.

C'uc'úpajc'ojam.

He pissed on it, ac'ój?am.

Séwdí, ma?át,

In the river, indeed,

p'op'óm osýdi,

he jumped on a clump of grass,

ma?át, týpt'ac'oj?am.

indeed, right there in the river, ac'ój?am.

Amádi, ma?at, hásc'oj?am.

There, indeed, he pissed, ac'ój?am.

Awéten bet'éksipweten,
yk'ójc'oj?am.

Thereupon he sprang out onto the bank,
he went away, ac'ój?am. (85)

Homóbokitmendi,
c'uc'úpajc'oj?am.

On every kind of thing there was,
he pissed, ac'ój?am.

Bewésc'oj?am

He scratched the ground with his hind feet,
ac'ój?am.

Ypék'ano hanódom,
býdam májdyk'i k'ódojnantedi,
ypék'ano hac'ónoc'oj?am.

Carrying everywhere,
even to the land of dangerous people,
everywhere wandering around, ac'ój?am.

Húmbotmenim dýdi, ypék'anbedi
c'uc'úpajdom, bewésdom,
hak'ójc'oj?am.

Wherever there were bushes, on all of them
he pissed on them, scratched the ground,
leaving his traces, ac'ój?am.

Ypék'ano hac'ónodom,
ékdadojkydi yc'ópinc'oj?am.

Wandering around everywhere,
he came to where the sun rises, ac'ój?am. (90)

Ámkanim,

After a while,

uním k'ódom ésto ypínc'oj?am.

he came to the Middle of the World, ac'ój?am.

Ypíndom,

Arriving,

uním K'ódom Ésto ymítkapinc'et,
májdyk'i mymý jáppatdojmenpe
ka?ántekitc'oj?am.

arriving at the very center of this land,
the people did not pursue him as far as that,
ac'ój?am.

Lithograph by Daniel Stolpe.

Ac'ét, anídi,
 mójdym wéjebosc'oj?am.
Ámkanim, ywájtoc'oj?am.

 Máwyk'ym jepónim mójdym,
  myk'í mójdyni,
  hehéj ?ynóc'oj?am.

Uním k'ódojdi, ypék'andykpem k'ódojdi,
  di wit'ípwajc'oj?am.

  Awéten, hatámc'oj?am.
  C'uc'úwonotic'oj?am.
  Pit'íwonotic'oj?am.
  Behéswonotic'oj?am.

 Ypék'andykpem k'ódojdi
  k'ódo ynóc'oj?am.
  Hatámkinuwebisim,
  as wónotic'oj?am.

 Ypék'anim k'ódom hatámdom,
wi?ítidom, hesíma?át c'eméndom,
   c'ebósdom,
jahátidom, hesí ma?át jac'émenwet,
 ypék'anlut'í mahámotoc'oj?am.

Mymým, Wépam Májdy, dónbosdom,
  hójwihamotoc'oj?am.

 Awéten myjím mójdym bomóm
ypék'anim wýkdi motólutweten,
  ynódojc'oj?am.

  Hójwihasitodom,
momím batásdi hójwihadiknoc'oj?am.
 Ámkanim hójwitanodom,

Meanwhile, then,
the people finished talking, ac'ój?am.
Afterwards, they went off in all directions, ac'ój?am.

Five of the leaders of the people,
along with their people,
set out in pursuit, ac'ój?am. (95)

In this world, everywhere in this world,
they traveled around, ac'ój?am.

Thereupon, looking, ac'oj?am.
For where he had pissed, ac'ój?am.
For where he had shat, ac'oj?am.
For where he had scratched the ground, ac'ój?am. (100)

Everywhere in this world,
they went to every place, ac'ój?am.
They kept searching them out,
destroying them, ac'ój?am.

Everywhere they searched the land,
going around, indeed missing none,
finding traces,
fixing it up well, cleaning it up well indeed;
they brought every single one together, ac'ój?am.

As for him, Coyote Person, they grabbed him
and brought him along with them, ac'oj?am.

Thereupon the many people,
having gathered together from everywhere,
set out as one, ac'ój?am. (105)

They brought him up to the banks of a river,
led him there, ac'ój?am.
Then leading him along,

ésto we?é aká,
nuktim ónkysdobe hukítweten,
bydójt'atic'oj?am.

close by the center,
having made a small island,
they made him sit on it, ac'ój?am.

"Unídi wónoma?amkano," ac'ój?am.
"Ypék'ani wewéjni tetét húkesjo?amkano,
amám unídi, okó wónodom,
wónoma?amkano!" ac'ój?am.

"Here you will die," ac'ój?am.
"You who are too clever with words,
so here, dying of hunger,
you will die!" ac'ój?am.

Amýni, "Héw," ac'oj?am.
"Ník,
mínsym jepónim májdym wónotidom,
mínsy dydýk'ym jepónjahanak'a,"
ac'ój?am.

Then, "Well!" ac'ój?am. (110)
"Me,
you leaders of the people are killing me,
you would have it that you alone shall lead,"
ac'ój?am.

"Níkdyk'y,
ypék'anbem k'ódojnan,
núkpapajmakyk 'an!" ka?ájcoj?am.

"I alone,
from each and every part of the world,
will be the one that they laugh at!" ac'ój?am.

"Adóm mín"
—mymým ka?án—
"ypék'anbem k'ódojnak, wasáj amápem:
'Húkeswalawpem!'
amák'an mín," ac'ój?am.

"And you,"
—turning to Him—
"from everywhere in the world, it will be bad:
'He is the cleverest!'
they will say of you," ac'ój?am.

Awéten, wewéjmenwet,
bísc'oj?am.

Thereupon, having spoken,
he remained silent, ac'ój?am.

Ac'ét yjéc'oj?am.
Yjéwebisim, haiyéwebism,
hasípc'oj?am.

Meanwhile the others went back, ac'ój?am. (115)
Kept returning, kept coming back,
came across to their starting point, ac'ój?am.

Amámk'an, "Sú," ac'oj?am.
"Ypék'andykbem, k'ódojdi mínsym,
pínhejjepada;
c'ýjim ekím wosípc'et,
mínsym pínmenmyni,
'wónobosdom' mamák'an," ac'ój?am.

Then, "Enough," ac'oj?am.
"All of you, wherever you are in this world,
listen well;
four days having passed,
you hear no sounds,
'He has died' you can say," ac'ój?am.

Lithograph by Daniel Stolpe.

Amýni májsem yk'ójc'oj?am.

Then they all went away, ac'ój?am.

Sýttim pó, bénekto, pínhejjec'et;
ac'ét, hónmaktinc'oj?am.

First night, by morning, they listened;
meanwhile, no sound from him, ac'ój?am. (120)

Béjbym, c'ájim bénekto,
pínhejjec'oj?am.
Ac'ét, hónmaktinc'oj?am.

Again, through the next morning,
they listened, ac'ój?am.
Meanwhile, there was no sound from him,
ac'ój?am.

Ac'ét, Wépam májdym húk'oj
bísc'oj?am.

Meanwhile, Coyote person still
remained quiet there, ac'ój?am.

Awéten, aját'an, pit'íc'oj?am.
Hemém onóm lýksipc'oj?am.
"Hesá mak'ádes?" ac'ój?am,
"Jahát ník japájtopi!" ac'ój?am.

Thereupon, after a while, he shat, ac'ój?am.
A gopher head crawled out, ac'ój?am. (125)
"What shall I do?" ac'ój?am.
"Speak to me well!" ac'ój?am.

"Hesámet ka?ámkano ypék'apedi
ejánwejat'an,
wónomapem," ac'ój?am.

"If you should just stay here
like you are,
you will die," ac'ój?am.

"A, ypék'anbenini ník ka?ámkano ka?ájpem,"
ac'ój?am.

"Ah, that's the way you always are to me,"
ac'ój?am.

Awéten hónkujat'an béjbym,
p'op'óm ok'ýnynim lýksipc'oj?am.
"Hesá mak'ádesi?" ac'ój?am.
"Hesánudom hónwejmak'adesi?" ac'ój?am.
"Jahát ník wéjepi!" ac'ój?am.

Thereupon, when he had strained again,
a bunch of dry grass crawled out, ac'ój?am. (130)
"What am I to do?" ac'ój?am.
"How shall I survive?" ac'ój?am.
"Speak to me well!" ac'ój?am.

"Hesámet ka?amkano, t'íwkitim
makýnodom?
k'ódom ékdakitdom,
t'íwdojdom, wýsdojnoc'et,
wýkkanuhadojnodom,
hasípmapem" ac'ój?am.

"Suppose that you make
yourself like mist?
when the sun rises,
as the mist rises, while it floats up,
mix with it as it is rising drifting along,
and thus you shall get across," ac'ój?am.

"Awéten, ka?ámkano pelípmapem,"
ac'ój?am.
"Anímmyni, mínk'i éstom

"Thereupon, suppose you call out,"
ac'ój?am. (135)
"Then, from the middle of the sandbar where,

Lithograph by Daniel Stolpe.

k'ýsdi maʔát c'uc'úwononimma,
behéswononimma,
p'op'óm osýdi maʔát
háswononimmam,
amám maʔát, kak'án mín pedátomapem,"
ac'ójʔam.

indeed, you have pissed,
you scratched up the ground,
indeed even a clump of grass
you have lifted your leg against,
then indeed, these places will answer you,"
ac'ójʔam.

Amýnik'an: "mým ápte ník maʔájkym,

tetét ník jahát wéjekym," ac'ójʔam.

And then: "he is the one who acts well
toward me,
he always speaks very well to me," ac'ójʔam.

"Ts'u'k-ts'u'k," ac'ójʔam.

"Ts'u'k-ts'u'k," ac'ójʔam.

Awéten, mykán hajác'ojʔam.

Thereupon, he stuck him back inside,
ac'ójʔam.

Awéten, myjím
Hemém onóni
k'adótc'ikc'ojʔam.

Thereupon, he plugged himself up with
Gopher head,
ac'ójʔam. (140)

Amám, k'ódom ékdojmadom,
banánakkitcet,
t'íwkim wýsdojc'ojʔam.
Ac'ét, wýkk'at'iwdojcojʔam.

Then, as the sun was rising,
it began to get light,
the mist floated up, ac'ójʔam.
Meanwhile, he mingled with the mist,
ac'ójʔam.

T'íwjewebisim, k'ydójmeninupe,
wýssipc'ojʔam.

As mist, he kept rising,
he floated across to the shore, ac'ójʔam.

Awéten, wat'á
týsbokitweten;
pelípdojc'ojʔam.
Amýni majákk'en hadána
pedátoc'jʔam.
Béjbym, 'ájna
pedátoc'ojʔam.

Thereupon, stopping in his tracks
on the river bank,
he called out, ac'ójʔam.
Then it seemed as if from far away
there was an answer, ac'ójʔam. (145)
Again, from somewhere else,
there was an answer, ac'ójʔam.

Myk'i c'umím, maʔat,
myk'í behéswonom, maʔát,
myk'í lýksipwonom, maʔát,
pedátoc'ojʔam.

His piss, indeed,
his scratching place, indeed,
his excrement, indeed,
they answered, ac'ójʔam.

Lithograph by Daniel Stolpe.

Amýni, mym májdym bomóm wéjecoj?am.   Then the people spoke, ac'ój?am.
    "Wónotibosmen, wónoky?enk'es así,"   "We killed, but did not kill all,"
                      ac'ój?am.   ac'ój?am.
                     "Myjím—   "He—
         mákpajpe mákpajdom—   having been instructed in what to do—
    c'yjím ekí pelípmenta," ac'ój?am.   four days he should not call out," ac'ój?am. (150)
    "Amám, ac'ét sáp'ym bénektom   "Now, while only three mornings have
                   wosípc'et,   passed,
               pelípc'oj?am."   he is calling out," ac'ój?am.

Amýni, májsem jék'ojtotoc'oj?am.   Then they went to one another, ac'ój?am.
    "Wónomenkyk'an así," ac'ój?am.   "He did not die," ac'ój?am.
       "Pelípk'an así," ac'ój?am.   "He is calling out," ac'ój?am.
   "Béjbym mínsy jáppatdoj," ac'ój?am.   "Again, you must pursue him," ac'ój?am. (155)

       "Ypék'anim k'ódojdi,   "From each and every part of the country,
   mínsym ýmmotopi," ac'ój?am.   you come together," ac'ój?am.
  "Wonóbene?e mínsym," ac'ój?am.   "You might lose him," ac'ój?am.
"Kaníwonom mákwonopi," ac'ój?am.   "Try to find him for the last time," ac'ój?am.

Amýnik'an jáppatdojc'oj?am.   And then they set out to track him down,
                           ac'ój?am. (160)

Ypék'andykbem k'ódojdi   Everywhere in the world
           ynóc'oj?am.   going along, ac'ój?am.
Ypék'anim ynówebisim k'an,   And going along everywhere,
  c'ajmen batámmotoc'oj?am.   they finally caught up with him, ac'ój?am.
    Ypék'anim majákk'en   And they brought together all kinds of things
 c'uc'úwono, bydójwonope,   from where he pissed, where he sat down,
   homó wokítmeni hés,   every sort of thing he had done,
      ypínmotoc'oj?am.   they brought together, ac'ój?am.

  Awéten tápo majákk'en,   Thereupon they captured him,
   májsem ynódojc'oj?am.   started off with him, ac'ój?am.

Tetém maják'ken c'á húkitc'oj?am.   They made a great tree grow, ac'ój?am. (165)
Amádi maják'ken bísc'oj?am.   They made him stand in the middle of it,
                            ac'ój?am.

   C'á ésto dímototic'oj?am.   They caused it to grow up around him,
                            ac'ój?am.

Amýni majákk'en týswejwebisc'oj?am.

Then the tree enclosed him as he stood,
ac'ój?am.

týsbokitweten dímototimyni.

enclosing him on all sides.

Awéten maják'ken májsem wéjec'ój?am.

Then they talked together, ac'ój?am.

"Su," ac'ój?am.

"Enough," ac'ój?am. (170)

"Kaním matá," ac'ój?am.

"Let this be an end to him," ac'ój?am.

"Uním nisé ónk'ojdom,
kaním mata," ac'ój?am.

"His getting the best of us,
let this be the end of it," ac'ój?am.

"Béjbym syk'álamentape?e,"
ac'ój?am.

"Let's not be bothered by him again,"
ac'ój?am.

"C'ýjim bénekto,
pelílipnomendom,
píntimapem kulúmyni,
'wónokyk'an, adóm,'
mínsym
japájtotokinuma?amkano," ac'ój?am.

"By the fourth morning,
if he has not called out,
making you hear him,
'he is dead, then,'
is what you will all tell each other
when it grows dark," ac'ój?am.

Awéten, májsem yk'ójk'ojc'oj?am.
Ypék'anbem k'ódojdi, pínhejjec'oj?am.

Having done so, they all went off, ac'ój?am. (175)
From every country, they listened, ac'ój?am.

Ac'étk'an, myná Mákmakkym
májdym
káj?okittec'oj?am.

And meanwhile Pileated Woodpecker
person came
flying by him, ac'ój?am.

Ámkanim myjím c'á bodátoc'oj?am.

He proceeded to tap near him on that tree,
ac'ój?am.

Bodátowebisim, bodátowebisim,
kulúmyni yk'ójc'oj?am.

He kept tapping, kept tapping.
when it grew dark he went away, ac'ój?am.

Béjbym, k'ódom ékdamyni,
káj?okíttec'oj?am.
Bodátowebisim, kulúmyni
yk'ójk'ojc'oj?am
Káj?okittec'oj?am

Again, at daybreak,
he came flying by, ac'ój?am. (180)
He kept tapping, when it grew dark,
he went off, ac'ój?am.
He flew away, ac'ój?am.

Lithograph by Daniel Stolpe.

Béjbym, k'ódom ékdamyni,
  káj?okíttec'oj?am.
Bodátowek'ojc'oj?am.
Bodátowebisim k'an myjí
  bek'élk'ojc'oj?am.
Webélbelc'oj?am.

Again, at daybreak,
he flew to that place, ac'ój?am.
He tapped, ac'ój?am.
And he kept tapping like that until
he had made a hole through it, ac'ój?am. (185)
He made a hole in it, ac'ój?am.

"Héw!" ac'ój?am.
"Popósim! Tetébe ma?át bek'él!"
  ac'ój?am.
Amýni k'an, k'elém bówetcn,
  kájk'ojwek'ojc'oj?am.
Káj?okítmenc'onoc'oj?am.

"Good!" ac'ój?am.
"Cousin! Make this hole a little bigger!"
ac'ój?am.
But then, stamping upon the hollow tree,
he flew away, ac'ój?am.
Not flying back again, ac'ój?am. (190)

"Tetét hap'á wasám ní!" ac'ój?am.
"Jahát jahámenim hap'á ní!" ac'ój?am.
"Hesámyni wewéjmenwet
  cenúmenjakk'esí?"
  ac'ój?am.

"I did very wrong!" ac'ój?am.
"I didn't do well at all!" ac'ój?am.
"Why didn't I just watch without saying
anything?"
ac'ój?am.

Awét k'an,
  tásc'oj?am.
Tássebisim k'an, myjím Hemém onóm
  lýksipc'oj?am.

And this having happened,
he strained, ac'ój?am.
And kept straining, until that Gopher head
crawled out, ac'ój?am. (195)

"Hesá mak'ádesí?" ac'ój?am.
"Jahát ník, hálmenwet, wéjepi," ac'ój?am.

"What am I going to do?" ac'ój?am.
"Speak well to me, don't lie," ac'ój?am.

Amýni k'an wéjec'oj?am.
"Hesámenwet ka?ámkano unídi
  ypék'anujat'an,
  wónomapem," ac'ój?am.

And then he spoke, ac'ój?am.
"There's nothing to do
but just to stay right here until
you die," ac'ój?am.

"Mí as ka?úsano, sýttini ma?át,
  jahát wéjemenpem,"
  ac'ój?am.
"Ypék'anbenini ka?ájkym!" ac'ój?am.

"You have never, not once, spoken well to
me!"
ac'ój?am. (200)
"You always talk this way!" ac'ój?am.

Awéten, sýttim bej
lýksipc'oj?am.
"Hesá mak'adesí?" ac'ój?am.
"Jahát ník wémt'ik'i wéje," ac'ój?am.

Thereupon, again another
crawled out, ac'ój?am.
"What shall I do?" ac'ój?am.
"Speak well to me all you can," ac'ój?am.

Amýni k'an , "Héw!" ac'ój?am.
"Hesámenwet ka?ámkano t'íwkim
makýnodom,
wysíjewebisim,
wysípbosmapem,"
ac'ój?am.
"Adóm, kaní ka?ánudom,
hónwenuma?amkano," ac'ój?am.

Then, "Well!" ac'ój?am. (205)
"There is nothing for you to do but make
like mist,
keep swishing through,
until you shall have swished outside,"
ac'ój?am.
"So, doing that,
you will survive," ac'ój?am.

Amýni k'an, "Héw!" ac'ój?am.
"Mi hápte ník ypék'anbenini
jahát wéjepem tené,"
ac'ój?am.

And so then, "Good!" ac'ój?am.
"You certainly
speak well to me every time,"
ac'ój?am.

Awéten,
wysíjec'oj?am.
Wysíwebisim k'an,
wysípbosc'oj?am.

Having so done,
he swished through, ac'ój?am. (210)
And he kept swishing,
until he had swished outside, ac'ój?am.

Amám k'an, ékdabosmadom,
kaním bénekto k'an,
pelípwek'ojc'oj?am.
K'ódom ékdajedom, jodádalc'opinc'et,
pelípwek'ojc'oj?am.

Thereupon, just about dawn
and on the last morning,
he called out, ac'ój?am.
As the sun rose, just as it was becoming light,
he called out, ac'ój?am.

Béjbym pedátowek'ojc'oj?am.
Ypékanbem k'ódojnan,
pelípwek' ojc'oj?am.
Awon'openjakan myj mác'oj?am.
Wépam, wo?ómyni,
pím jákwejto
betéjtodi,
myk'í c'uc'úwonom, ma?át,
myk'í behéswonom, ma?át,

Again, they called back to him, ac'ój?am.
From every part of the land,
they called out, ac'ój?am. (215)
It seemed like this at the time, mác'oj?am.
Coyote, to his howling,
when it seems many things could talk,
in ancient times,
where he had left piss, indeed,
where he had left scratchings, indeed,

Lithograph by Daniel Stolpe.

myk'í wypýpylamtowonom maʔát,
lýksipwonom,
myk'í awónopem maʔát,
pedátom, májc'ojʔam.
Amám, bomóm
májcojʔam — béj —
Ac'ék woʔómyni howáwadom,
pím jákwejto mym bomóm maʔat.

Amýni k'an, béjbym wéjec'ojʔam.
"Jepónim májdy k'ódom jywátokynan;
ník mínsym c'enóʔokitti," ac'ójʔam.
Amýni k'an, myk'í májdy
jék'ojc'ojʔam.
Yk'ójdom k'an,
ypék'anim k'ódojdi wéjek'ojdom,
wéjeʔysipc'ojʔam.

Awéten k'an,
jewéjc'ojʔam.
Adóm k'an okítweten,
bísc'et,
okíkitc'ojʔam.
Okíttebisim, okíttebisim,
uním c'ám
jamánim jákbec'ojʔam.

K'ódom ékdamyni wéjec'ojʔam.
"Tújc'enok'a, mínsym" ac'ójʔam.
"Ypékanim mínsym,
tújc'enok'a," ac'ójʔam.
"Pínk'enup mínsym wéjesi,"
ac'ójʔam.

"Uním k'ódom k'adíkmak'an," ac'ójʔam.
"Kómak'an," ac'ójʔam.
"Awét, kómak'an," ac'ójʔam.
"Ypék'anim k'ódo,
mómbudutc'onotimak'an,"
ac'ójʔam.

where he had rolled over and over, indeed,
where something had crawled out of him,
where all those things were, indeed,
they answered him, majc'ójʔam.
And it sounded like a lot of them,
majc'ójʔam — again —
About this time, responding to his howling,
it seemed like there were many indeed.

And so then, he spoke again, ac'ójʔam. (220)
"Go visit the leaders throughout the land;
invite them to come to me," ac'ójʔam.
And so then his people
went to invite them, ac'ójʔam.
And going about,
speaking of it in every country,
they spoke there, ac'ójʔam.

And having done so,
they came back, ac'ójʔam.
And then they kept arriving,
one after another,
they arrived, ac'ójʔam. (225)
They kept coming, kept coming,
until they seemed as
many as the trees on the mountain, ac'ójʔam.

At sunrise he spoke, ac'ójʔam.
"Wake up, you all," ac'ójʔam.
"Each and every one of you,
wake up," ac'ójʔam.
"Listen now to what I have to say,"
ac'ójʔam. (230)

"There shall be rain in this world," ac'ójʔam.
"There shall be snow," ac'ójʔam.
"But it shall really snow," ac'ójʔam.
"All over the land,
the water shall be made to rise,"
ac'ójʔam.

Lithograph by Daniel Stolpe.

"Mik'í májdy, mínsym
jak'á tawálma?amkano,"
ac'ój?am.
"T'íkpinma?amkano ník mínsym," ac'ój?am.
"Wíjjemenmak'an!" ac'ój?am.

"My people, you all
must build a boat,"
ac'ój?am. (235)
"You must believe what I tell you," ac'ój?am.
"It shall not fail to be so!" ac'ój?am.

"Wémt'ik'i ka?ájk'as, wejedom,
k'ódom k'adíkmak'an," ac'ój?am.

"Having said enough, so I have spoken,
there shall be rain in this world," ac'ój?am.

"Uním jamánmanto mómbudutk'ojmyni,
Wépam pájdym wi?ímak'an," ac'ój?am.
"Ac'ét, mínsydyk'ym, nik'í májdym
hónwe?ima?amkano," ac'ój?am.

"All these mountains deep under water,
Coyote person will be destroyed," ac'ój?am.
"However, you alone, my people,
shall survive," ac'ój?am. (240)

Amýni, "Héw!" ac'ój?am.

So then, "Good!" ac'ój?am.

Jak'á sikésc'oj?am,
Sikésc'ój?am.

They prepared the boat, ac'ój?am.
They prepared it, ac'ój?am.

Wépam májdym c'ájt'ikkadom,
Wépam jákc'etimendom,
uním májdym
bomók'an tétec'oj?am.
Amýni k'an, májsem mákkitmenc'oj?am.

Coyote person, disguising himself,
not looking like Coyote,
this man
mingled with lots of people, ac'ój?am.
So then they didn't recognize him,
ac'ój?am. (245)

Jawébisim, sýttim k'úmmeni wosípc'oj?am.
Jak'á c'ómenpe,
tawálc'oj?am.
Myk'í májdym tawálc'oj?am.

Kept making it, one winter passed, ac'ój?am.
The boat not yet burnt out,
they worked, ac'ój?am.
His people worked, ac'ój?am.

K'úmmemenkitpot'oc'et,
c'ópotoc'oj?am.
Ac'et, k'ódom kóc'oj?am.
Sikésc'oj?am.
Sikéssebisim,
k'ódom kadíkc'oj?am.
Pénem k'ùmmen tawáldom,
tawálbosc'oj?am.

Another winter,
it was almost burnt out, ac'ój?am.
Although it snowed, ac'ój?am.
They worked at it, ac'ój?am. (250)
As they stuck to the task,
it began again to rain, ac'ój?am.
When they had worked through two winters,
the task was done, ac'ój?am.

Lithograph by Daniel Stolpe.

"Ókk'etwonopem, mínsy," ac'ój?am.
Amýni k'an, "Héw!" ac'ój?am.
"Wépam májdym okítbyny?y;
mínsym ókk'etwonopi," ac'ój?am.

"Be on the alert, all of you," ac'ój?am.
And so then, "Well!" ac'ój?am. (255)
"Coyote person might show up;
you must always be on guard," ac'ój?am.

Amýni k'an, "Héw!" ac'ój?am.
"Tetét c'ekátam asi," ac'ój?am.
Wépam májc'oj?am.
Ac'ét, mymý c'esákmenc'oj?am.

And so then, "Well!" ac'ój?am.
"I'll watch very closely," ac'ój?am.
It was Coyote who spoke, májc'oj?am.
However, the others didn't recognize him,
ac'ój?am. (260)

"Wépa ka?ás c'esákmapem," ac'ój?am.
"Mym okítk'an, amápem kak'ás," ac'ój?am.
Wépam, ma?át, majc'oj?am.

"I can recognize Coyote," ac'ój?am.
"If he comes, I'll tell you," ac'ój?am.
It was Coyote, indeed, who spoke, ac'ój?am.

Amýni k'an, "Héw!" ac'ój?am.

And then, "Good!" ac'ój?am.

K'ódom k'adikc'oj?am.
Momím mómbomitc'oj?am.
Hybódi opítc'oj?am.
Jákdi, májsem híndojc'oj?am.

It rained in the world, ac'ój?am. (270)
Water flowed in, ac'ój?am.
It flooded the houses, ac'ój?am.
In the boat, they began to float, ac'ój?am.

"Hesá mínsym píkno mak'á?" ac'ój?am.
"Wépam yhéjmenk'ade?" ac'ój?am.
Amýni: "he?é," ac'ój?am.
"Niséwet píkno ka?émk'es," ac'ój?am.

"Are you the only ones here?" ac'ój?am.
"Coyote isn't here, is he?" ac'ój?am. (275)
So then: "yes," ac'ój?am.
"Only we ourselves are here," ac'ój?am.

Híndojcoj?am.
Ac'ét, k'ódom kadíkc'oj?am.
Ypék'anim jamánmanto k'an
mómbudutc'onoc'oj?am.
k'ódom mómdom.

It floated up, ac'ój?am.
Meanwhile, it rained in the world, ac'ój?am.
All of the mountains were
covered by water, ac'ój?am, (280)
water just filled it up.

Amýni k'an: mydí, májsem,
hínsitojewebisim,
k'ódo c'ec'oj?am.
Adóm k'an: mydí,
májsem hasípc'oj?am,

And so then: him,
the people kept floating around
until they saw land, ac'ój?am.
And then: him, they
pushed along the surface of the water,
ac'ój?am,

Lithograph by Daniel Stolpe.

Jakúkim Jamándi.	to Canoe Mountain [also known as Keddie Peak].
Adóm k'an,	Then, having pushed
hasípmyni,	along the surface of the water,
"á! ní uním k'ódo c'és!" ac'ój?am.	"yes! I'm the one who saw this land!" ac'ój?am.
Amýni k'an, myjím tetém májdym	And so then, that great person,
c'ekákasipweten, oléli c'edóm,	taking a long look, seeing the coyote,
bísc'oj?am—wewéjmenwet—	stayed there, ac'ój?am—not saying anything—
Mydí k'an, myjím Wépam májdym	And so Coyote person
lýkmitc'et,	had slipped in,
májsem ypék'anim májdym	while all of the people
c'esákmenwonokyc'oj?am.	had not recognized him, ac'ój?am. (285)
"Tetét ka?ámkano éptidom,	"You have astonishing power,
amám t'íkbe mín húntas," ac'ój?am.	though I have hunted you enough," ac'ój?am.
"Ebým mín wónotimawet,	"For a long time trying to kill you,
wónotic'yjk'as:	I have failed to kill you:
onk'oj?amkano ník," ac'ój?am.	you have defeated me," ac'ój?am.
Ac'ét k'an, mym, bet'éksipim,	And meanwhile, he, having jumped out,
kýswowopini,	down along the ridge,
jác'aj ?ýnpinc'oj?am.	came trotting along, ac'ój?am.
Amýni ka'n,	And so then:
"mínsyk'i ynójahape ynópada,"	"all of you go wherever you wish,"
acój?am.—myk'í májdy—	ac'ój?am.—to his people—
Ámkanim k'an, ynódojim kaním,	And then afterwards, he set out hence
myná ýnnoc'oj?am.	and went away from them, ac'ój?am. (290)
Ámkanim k'an, obýnona,	And then, afterward,
bísc'oj?am.	he crossed south from there, ac'ój?am.
Mydí wojím. kaním.	He remained. That is all.

SIX

Hybýkʼym Masý Wónom / Love and Death

Hybýkʼym Masý Wónom	Love and Death
"Mymým, Wépam májdym, hapónkʼojtiʔuscʼykʼan."	"He, Coyote person, seems to defeat himself."
"Amét, haʔáj ní wónom májdykʼi núkdom, jahát hybýkdom, ekʼawcʼeʔusmape wéjekʼas," acʼójʔam. "Kylóknon kíw," acʼójʔam.	"On the contrary, it is I who speak for mortal man's laughter, contentment, and delight in themselves," acʼójʔam. "Women too," acʼójʔam.

Acʼek kʼan, myjím májdym ypékʼanu hakʼójdom ykʼójcʼojʔam, Ékdadojkym kʼódojdi ycʼónodom, ypékʼano hacʼónodom, wýnnynykʼopindom, ypékʼano hapíndom komódi; adóm, ypíncʼojʔam.	Meanwhile, that person was continually going along farther away, acʼójʔam. He went over to the land where the day begins, and always going up and over the ridges, he circled back this way, moving ever southward; then he got closer, acʼójʔam.
Amám so yjém kʼan myjim mymý wasópajwonom májdydi okítcʼojʔam. Acʼék, kyléni bíscʼojʔam.	Thereupon he came at last to that person who had been angry with him, acʼójʔam. At the time, he was living with his wife, acʼójʔam.
"Héw, niksámbojem, kylékym wasátimadi kawéʔano, kylécʼoni bísdom," acʼójʔam. "Hesádom mín májdymenim jákkype maʔát,	"Well, my brother, you seem to be headed for a bad marriage, living with a wife," acʼójʔam. (5) "How is it that a good-looking woman

Intaglio by Daniel Stolpe.

wasám c'etípem májdy maʔát
mín kylóknonom
ek'áwc'edom mak'áde,
jépkydom?" ac'ójʔam.
Amýni: "Ní, jahátc'etipem májdym maʔát,
kyle wiʔídom!" ac'ójʔam.

would come to marry an ugly person
like you
who doesn't even look
like a man?" ac'ójʔam.
So then: "Here I am, a handsome man,
without a wife!" ac'ójʔam.

Awéten, bísʔidic'ojʔam.

And then, he moved in with them, ac'ójʔam.

"Kylé ník hesápediwet,
méj maʔ amkano," ac'ójʔam.
"Ní as kaʔúsas tetét hóntosdom:
tújdom, ník sykálac'et,
kak'ás t'ijýkmenweú
tújkym, kylék'an tújhojjedom," ac'ójʔam.

"If you can find a woman anywhere,
give her to me," ac'ójʔam.
"I have always had great willpower:
the first time I sleep with two women
and they start playing around with me,
I won't move a muscle!" ac'ójʔam.

"Adóm, kaʔámkano,
bénekto kylék'an tújc'enomapem," ac'ójʔam.
"Amám, c'ájim pótapo,
kaʔámkano sykálajahadom,
sykálamapem," ac'ójʔam.

"Then if you do that, you'll wake up in the
morning with wives," ac'ójʔam. (10)
"Thereupon, all the next night,
if you want to bother them,
you can just go ahead and do it," ac'ójʔam.

"Ní kak'ás t'ijýkmenmapem!" ac'ójʔam.

"I will not move!" declared Coyote, ac'ójʔam.

Amam k'an, poʔestoc'et,
pénem jálulu
jymýʔasitoweten,
inʔánto wokítc'ojʔam.

And thereupon, in the middle of the night,
he [K'ódojapem] carried two elderberry flutes
across,
and laid them alongside him [Wépam],
ac'ójʔam.

K'an ékdapotoc'et,
"hn, hn,"
awéjc'ojʔam.
Myjím k'an mymy sykálamyni,
sykásajtoc'ojʔam.

Then when it was almost daybreak,
"hn, hn,"
he woke up and snickered, ac'ójʔam.
And having messed around with each,
he messed around with both together,
ac'ójʔam. (15)

Amám k'an, bénekto,
myjím kyléc'om wiʔíc'ojʔam.

Thereupon, when daylight came,
the two women had disappeared, ac'ójʔam.

Intaglio by Daniel Stolpe.

Amýni k'an: "Wépam hap'á ní, tetét hésna
maʔát jahámenpem!
Tetét wasám májdym!
Hesámyni nik
wéjepe t'ikc'emenjakk'esʔ" ac'ójʔam.

So then: "Indeed I, Coyote, am no good for
anything at all!
A very bad man!
Why don't I believe it when
somebody tells me something?" ac'ójʔam.

"T'íkc'edom haʔáj,
tetét jaháhudojk'as," ac'ójʔam.
"Adóm kaʔás kyléwiʔídom," ac'ójʔam.
"Béjbym kaʔámenmak'as!
Ypék'anbe wewéj
t'ikc'emak'as!" ac'ójʔam.

"If I had believed,
everything would be fine," ac'ójʔam.
"But now I'm without a wife," ac'ójʔam.
"I won't do it again!
I'll believe what anybody tells
me!" ac'ójʔam. (20)

Amám k'an bisc'ojʔam.
Humbotmenim symí, wátky,
kaʔápepek'an,
wónotidom, pedóm, bísc'ojʔam.

So they stayed there, ac'ójʔam.
Hunting all kinds of deer, ducks,
anything to eat,
killing them, eating them, they stayed there,
ac'ójʔam.

K'an hunmok'ojmadom,
pándaka myk'í jahahátiweten, yk'ojc'ojʔam.

Then he [K'ódojapem] was going hunting,
got his bow ready and left, ac'ójʔam.

Ac'ét, Wépam májdym bísc'ojʔam.

However, Coyote person stayed home,
ac'ójʔam.

Ac'ét, uním tetém májdym
mákkitmenc'ojʔam.
C'esákmenc'oj ʔam—
mymým Wépam májdym
majákk'en—
Adóm buhejjec'et:
"Wépammenim" jákkac'ojʔam.
Amýni: "Hesápem k'ódojnanweí,
k'ódo maʔát hatámdom, ynójepem
majákk'en,"
ájk'ak'at'atc'ojʔam.

However, when this great person
came back, ac'ójʔam,
He didn't know the other, ac'ójʔam—
he didn't
recognize him as Coyote person—
Then he pondered:
"That doesn't look like Coyote," ac'ójʔam.
So then: "This fellow must have come from
somewhere or other, wandering around,
looking for a place to live,"
he thought ac'ójʔam.

Adóm, húhejhejnomenc'ojʔam.

Then he didn't think any more about it,
ac'ójʔam.

Amám k'an májc'om bísc'oj?am.

They both stayed there, ac'új?am. (30)

Majhí humíndom, bísc'oj?am.

They lived by netting salmon, ac'új?am.

Májdym ýmmotodom, bísc'oj?am.

Other people came and lived there, ac'új?am.

Amádi k'an, sýttim májdym okítc'oj?am.

From thence, a stranger came along, ac'új?am.

Amýni k'an, makó, majhí ítusweten, méjc'oj?am.

And so, when they had roasted salmon, they gave him some, ac'új?am.

Amýni k'an, pec'új?am.

And so then he ate it, ac'új?am. (35)

Pejat'an, c'ájmen týskadojim kaním, ynóc'oj?am.

And later, when he had finished eating, he got up and went away, ac'új?am.

K'an kýpjetidom pedóm, héjjujetipe;

And he dropped some food, leaving it behind;

"Héw! Makó wahénodom, pekýk'an!" ac'új?am.

"Look here! Wasting fish, this is how he ate!" ac'új?am.

Ám kaním myjím májdom byjýkdojdom, pec'új?am.

And gathering up the remains that this man had abandoned, he ate it, ac'új?am.

Wépam: "Á nik'í!" ac'új?am.

Coyote: "Oh my!" ac'új?am.

"Jahát wené ma?át sudákk'ade!" ac'új?am.

"This is very good indeed!" ac'új?am.

"Tené mínsym dómaki," ac'új?am.

"Everyone take a taste," ac'új?am. (40)

Adóm, sýtti hápnoc'oj?am.

He handed bits of it around to one person, ac'új?am.

Sýtti béjbym hápnoc'oj?am.

He handed bits of it to another, ac'új?am.

"Makókan," ac'új?am.

"The fish," ac'új?am.

"Tetét lut'í sudákkyk'an," ac'új?am.

"It is wonderful," ac'új?am. (45)

"Bám majdym kakýk'an!" ac'új?am.

"That was Salt person!" ac'új?am.

"Bínmejdojpe?e wónotiwejdom!" ac'új?am.

"Let's all go chase him down and kill him!" ac'új?am.

Án kaním, bínmedojc'oj?am.

Finished, they chased him, ac'új?am.

Wilékk'ojc'oj?am.

They went quickly, ac'új?am.

Pájdi pahéjk'ojc'oj?am.

They followed his tracks, ac'új?am.

Intaglio by Daniel Stolpe.

Béjdyk ynópem maʔát,	Even though he had just then left,
c'etímenc'ojʔam.	they couldn't find him, ac'ójʔam. (50)
Héjk'ojc'ojʔam.	They followed on, ac'ójʔam.
"Tóttimenweti!" ac'ójʔam.	"Call on all your power!" ac'ójʔam.
"Tóttimenwet! Bínmedoj!" ac'ójʔam.	"Do your best! Stay after him!" ac'ójʔam.
Amýni bínmek'ojc'ojʔam.	And so they went in pursuit, ac'ójʔam.
"Tókdaby'ʔy nisé!" ac'ójʔam.	"He might outrun us!" ac'ójʔam. (55)
"Motápaj!" ac'ójʔam.	"Go for him!" ac'ójʔam.
"Héjnopi mí nsym!" ac'ójʔam.	"Keep after him you people!" ac'ójʔam.
"Tóttimenwet mí nsym bínmedoj!" ac'ójʔam.	"Do the best you can, chase him!" ac'ójʔam.
Jamandi bylékwodojdom,	They ran up to the top of a mountain,
c'ehéjwokitc'ojʔam.	looked all around, ac'ójʔam.
Wiʔíc'ojʔam.	He was not there, ac'ójʔam. (60)
C'eménc'ojʔam.	They could not see him, ac'ójʔam.
"Túttimeweti!" ac'ójʔam.	"Keep after him with all your strength!" ac'ójʔam.
"Wasájadom nisé majákk'en:	"He might get the best of us:
Tóttimenwet! Mínsym bínmedoj!" ac'ójʔam.	Try your best! Stay after him!" ac'ójʔam.
Witóminodom jamándi	They ran down the first mountain
bylékwodojdom,	and up another one,
c'ehéjwonomyni,	and when they had taken a look around,
hésmen aním kojóna ýtnoc'ojʔam.	they went down into the valley below, ac'ójʔam.
Uním tetém c'á, waláwdykbedom,	This stranger, just high above the trees,
hadá aní wodíknoweten ynócojʔam.	was far away and running, ac'ójʔam. (65)
Amýni: "Héw!" ac'ójʔam.	So then: "Good!" ac'ójʔam.
"Tóttimenwet!	"Stretch yourselves to the limit!
Bínmedoj!	Stay after him!
Tókdadom nisé kakýk'an!"	He seems to be getting away from us!"
ac'ójʔam.	ac'ójʔam.

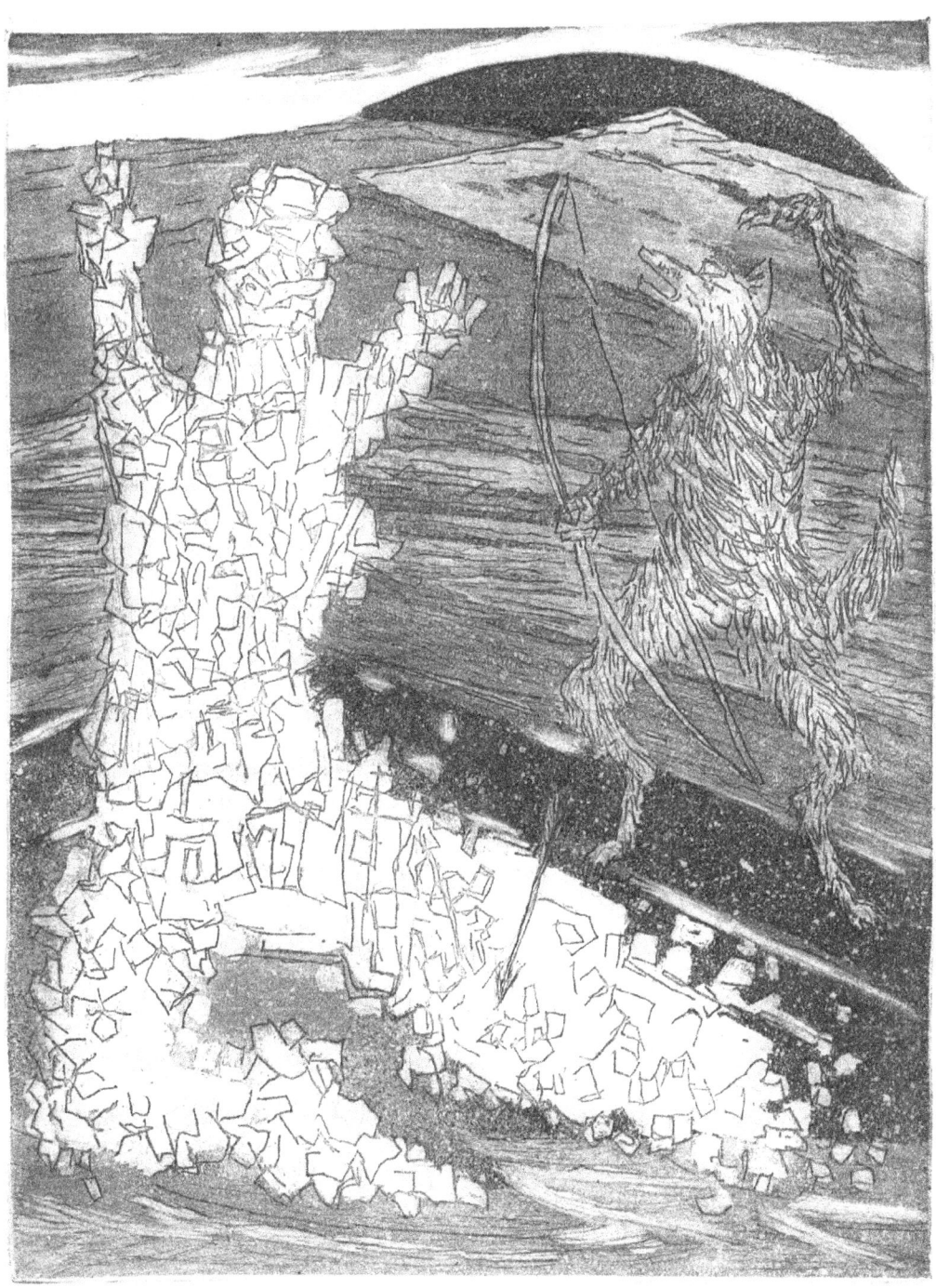

Intaglio by Daniel Stolpe.

Béjdyk ejápem kýsdo
obýʔasc'onopem maʔát,
kaʔánte hójpaj wodáwtikyk'an,
ac'ójʔam.

"And now it does indeed appear
as if he's gone further over the ridge;
he appears to have left them far behind,"
ac'ójʔam.

Uním Wépam bomó tókdadom, mac'ójʔam.
"Tóttimenweti!" ac'ójʔam.
Bínmek'ojc'ojʔam.

This Coyote outran everyone else, mac'ójʔam.
"Do the best you can!" ac'ójʔam. (70)
They were all in hot pursuit, ac'ójʔam.

Kojóm wat'á witýmic'ojʔam.

They came to the edge of the valley,
ac'ójʔam.

Ac'ét, aním hésmen ysítoc'ojʔam.

But the stranger had already run across it,
ac'ójʔam.

"Tóttimenweti!" ac'ójʔam.
"Tókdabyʔy nisé!" ac'ójʔam.
"Tóttimenweti!" ac'ójʔam.

"Use your power!" ac'ójʔam.
"He may outrun us yet!" ac'ójʔam. (75)
"Use your power!" ac'ójʔam.

Kojóm ésto towojkitc'et
yk'ójc'ojʔam.
"Héw, tókdadom haʔáj nisé kakýk'an!"
ac'ójʔam.

He reached the middle of the valley,
ac'ójʔam.
"Now, let's see if he beats us!"
ac'ójʔam.

Wépam, majákk'en,
mýc'ojʔam.
Syʔáʔasdojweten, támleptidom majákk'en,
jodúkdom tolím kámosi mýc'ojʔam.

Coyote, raising his bow,
send the arrow fast, ac'ójʔam.
Shooting low, he hit him in the calf
of the leg, ac'ójʔam. (80)

Mýmyni, majákk'en ypék'anu,
hánnodom, hejúnodom,
wohóholoc'ojʔam.

He, pierced by that arrow,
still went on, falling,
broken all to pieces, ac'ójʔam.

Bám Jépsabe k'an
Wépam wónotic'ojʔam.

Wild-man Salt
was killed by Coyote, ac'ójʔam.

Awéten k'an,
yk'ójdom májsem
ydíknoc'ojʔam.
Awéten k'an, Wépam wéjec'ojʔam:

Meanwhile,
all the other people caught up to him,
ac'ójʔam.
Having done this, Coyote spoke to them,
ac'ójʔam:

"'Betéjmen k'an myjím Wépam
Bám Nenó wónotipaʔajk'an,
myk'í májdy tókdabosc'et;'"
amápem kaʔán
wónom májdym, wéjedom," ac'ójʔam.

"Amána k'an, bá, komóna bádom,
unína bá hýʔokitmapem;
wónom májdym
k'ódom t'iknan,"
ac'ójʔam.
"Adóm k'an unína yjémápem,"
ac'ójʔam.
"Uním k'an, wónom májdyk'i
bám mamápem,"
ac'ójʔam

Adóm k'an wéjec'ojʔam.
Awéten k'an, jewéjc'ojʔam.

Yjéwebisim
mykánim k'ódojdi
yjéwebisim mysék'i yk'ójwonom bódi
yjéwebisim, okítc'ojʔam.

Awetén k'an,
majhí humínhekitdom,
ywájkitc'ojʔam.

Amám k'an, myjím jepónim
wéjec'ojʔam:
"Uním pím k'ùtíyt'ym, c'ajc'ajnom májdym,
wasák'an," ac'ójʔam.
"Pí wónotidom wasák'an,"
ac'ójʔam.
"Amaná ynómak'as,"
ac'ójʔam.

Ac'ét Wépam wewéjmenwet, bísc'ojʔam.

"'In ancient times that Coyote
killed Old Man Salt,
after he had outrun everybody else';
This is what
mortal people will say," ac'ójʔam. (85)

"Henceforth, to gather their salt, coming
here from everywhere for salt,
mortal people
shall come hither,"
ac'ójʔam.
"Henceforth this is where they'll come,"
ac'ójʔam.
"From here on out, mortal people
shall have Salt,"
ac'ójʔam.

And so he spoke to them, ac'ójʔam.
Having done so, they turned back,
ac'ójʔam. (90)

They kept traveling
on their old familiar trails,
kept traveling until they got there,
kept traveling, and then they stopped,
ac'ójʔam.

Having done so,
and having finished netting fish,
they went their separate ways, ac'ójʔam.

Another time later, this leader
spoke, ac'ójʔam:
"To have all these many creatures, all these
different kinds of people," is bad ac'ójʔam.
"It's bad because they kill one another,"
ac'ójʔam. (95)
"Because of this, I shall send them away,"
ac'ójʔam.

But Coyote remained there, silent, ac'ójʔam.

Intaglio by Daniel Stolpe.

"Uním k'ùtt'ym májdym wiʔíbosmyni kak'án,
c'ájim bísmak'an uním k'ódojdi,"
ac'ójʔam.
"Uním k'ùtt'ym májdym
pí wónotitodom,
jahámenk'an!" ac'ójʔam.
"Amám, mý hékitmak'an!" ac'ójʔam.

"If all these bird people were all gone,
then some others would live in this land,"
ac'ójʔam.
"That all these bird people
are killing each other!"
ac'ójʔam.
"It must stop!" ac'ójʔam. (100)

Ac'ét Wépam wewéjmenc'ojʔam.

But Coyote said nothing, ac'ójʔam.

Sýttim mac'ójʔam,
Tét'yt'ykypem p'ýbe, tetém p'ýbe;
amá lýksiptimenwet,
bístik'ijepem
mac'ójʔam—tetét jahát—

He had one child, mac'ójʔam.
He had a boy, a big boy;
and he never let him go out,
always made him stay at home,
mac'ójʔam—that was the way it was—

Amám k'an:
"wónom májdym, jakýpem májdym,
bísmak'an,"
ac'ójʔam.
"Wónom májdy mamák'an, ac'ójʔam.
Amám májdym kaían kylékytojahadom,
kylékytomapem, ac'ójʔam.
"Awét k'an, kylémaʔát
hesátimenwet kylékymak'an,"
ac'ójʔam.

And thereupon:
"mortal people, people with names,
will live here,"
ac'ójʔam.
"There will be mortal people," ac'ójʔam. (105)
"And when a man wants to have a wife,
he will have a wife," ac'ójʔam.
"However, when they are married,
he won't do anything with his wife,"
ac'ójʔam.

Amýni Wépam wewéjc'ojʔam.
Pédatonwet bísjet:

So then Coyote finally spoke up, ac'ójʔam.
And he answered him:

"Mý kaʔámkano wasáwejedom!" ac'ójʔam.

"That which you say is bad!" ac'ójʔam.

"Hesádom, mak'á jepónim májdym,
wónom májdyk'i kylék'an
maʔát sykásajtodom,
núkdom, jahát hybýkdom amápe,
májmenmapem?"
ac'ójʔam.

"Why, great leader
to mortal men and women:
that they may mess around
laughing and feeling happy,
will you not grant them this?"
ac'ójʔam. (110)

Intaglio by Daniel Stolpe.

"Wónom májdym haʔáj kylékytodom,
amýni héjjetodom,
t'íktena,
jok'óstonudom haʔáj,
kak'án tetét jahát hybýkmapem!
awéten, hékitdom,
kak'án jahát,
nùkdom, japájtotomapem,"
ac'ójʔam.
"Amét haʔáj, sikálatotomenwet,
tújdom,
wasópajtotom jákkanudom,
wasák'an,"
ac'ójʔam.
"Kaʔámenmapem kak'án!" ac'ójʔam.

Ac'ét, jepónim, wewéjmenwet,
pínk'enuc'ojʔam.
Wéjebosmyni,
béjby wéjec'ojʔam.

"Wónom májdym, kaʔán tét'yt'y kymádom,
kyjáhadom, p'ýbe maʔát kyjáhadom,
jawíweten,
myc'ó ésto
jymýkitmapem,"
ac'ójʔam.
"'Kylém p'ýbem mamáʔamkano,'
awéten ... ,"
ac'ójʔam.
"Améndom ma'at:
'p'ýbem mamáʔamkano,'
awéten ... ," ac'ójʔam.
"Myk'í kyjáhape jawíweten
jymýkitpem kaʔán,
bénekto tùjc'enomapem,
tibímenim, wémt'ik'i hukespem,"
ac'ójʔam.

"When mortal people are married,
they should make love,
and then, a little later,
they should lie down together,
and feel good!
and then, when they have finished
lovemaking,
they should laugh a lot and talk to each other,"
ac'ójʔam.
"But if, without messing with each other,
they sleep,
it will seem as if they were angry with each
other, and that would be bad,"
ac'ójʔam.
"It's just not going to be that way!" ac'ójʔam.

Meanwhile, the leader did not speak,
he listened, ac'ójʔam.
When the other had finished speaking,
he spoke again, ac'ójʔam. (115)

"Mortal people, in order to have children,
indeed wishing, wishing to have a child,
naming their desire,
they will lay something down
between them,"
ac'ójʔam.
"'You're going to be a girl-child,'
having done so ... ,"
ac'ójʔam.
"Or alternately:
'you're going to be a boy-child,'
having done so ... ," ac'ójʔam.
"When they have said what it is to be
and have laid it down between them,
then when they wake up in the morning,
[it will be] not small, and sufficiently clever,"
ac'ójʔam.

"Amýni, ka?án kylóknonom,
  wasá hybýkmenwet,
  tét'yt'y ky?ýjemapem," ac'ój?am.

"So then, it shall be that women,
not suffering,
will go about having children," ac'ój?am. (120)

Ac'ét, Wépam, wewéjmenwet,
  pínk'enuc'oj?am.
  Wéjebosmyni,
  mymý béj wéjec'oj?am:

However, Coyote saying nothing,
listened, ac'ój?am.
When the other had finished speaking,
again he spoke, ac'ój?am:

"Wónom májdym kylóknonom ka?án té
  yhájedom,
  amýni wákdom, tásdom, awébisim;
  ka?án wi?ínit, tét'yt'y kymápem,"
    ac'ój?am.
"Améndom ka?án léjwom wónomapem,
  amýni ka?án léjwom hónwe?imapem,"
    ac'ój?am.

"When mortal women wish to have a child,
then they will do so
groaning, weeping, straining;
and after a while, they may have the child,"
ac'ój?am.
"Sometimes some of them will die.
And then some of them will live,"
ac'ój?am.

Ac'ét, tetém májdym béjby wéjec'oj?am:

However, the great person spoke again:

"Hálbisim kylóknonom ka?án jépkydom
  dyk'ý jéptik'an wýkdi motómapem,"
    ac'ój?am.
"Amýni, ka?án kyléwi?ipem májdym
  kylékydom dyk'ý kylék'an
  tùjkitmapem," ac'ój?am.
  Ac'ój?am, tetém májdym.

"Maidens will come together with men
only after they are married,"
ac'ój?am. (125)
"And men who do not have women
will sleep with women
only once they are married," ac'ój?am.
Ac'ój?am, the great person said.

Ac'ét, Wépam wéjedojc'oj?am:

However, Coyote started to speak, ac'ój?am.

"Jepíwi?ipem kylém ma?át ka?án
  hálbis tékydom, amýni tékymapem,"
    ac'ój?am.

"Indeed, women without husbands and
maidens, they will have children,"
ac'ój?am.

"Wépam c'umí bénc'onowonokyk'an,
  hálbis tékydom;
  adóm ka?án wónom májdym:
  jépsym májdym, kylóknono c'ewéjdom,
  núkdom, wéjemapem,

"By stepping across Coyote's piss,
maidens will have children;
and then among mortal persons:
young men will gaze at women,
laughing, talking,

Intaglio by Daniel Stolpe.

p'ýt'yt'ym májdym wýkdi motódom,"
ac'ój?am.

when young people get together,"
ac'ój?am. (130)

"Jep'í wi?ipem kylém ma?át
bódi héjjeto ynójedom,
tét'yt'ypem kylém; amám:
kylém té apánojemyni,
amýni ka?án, p'ýt'yt'ym májdym núkdom,
wéjedom,
tetét jahát hybýkmapem," ac'ój?am.
Ac'ój?am, Wépam.

"And women without husbands,
making love along the trails,
will have children; and following upon this:
if such a woman carries her child about,
then young people will be smiling,
talking,
they will feel very happy," ac'ój?am.
Ac'ój?am, Coyote.

Myjím tetém májdym béjby wéjec'oj?am.

This great man spoke again, ac'ój?am:

"Wónom májdym wónodom,
amýni wónoc'et
wowóhac'onodom séwdi;
wowóc'onomyni,
mamák'an hónwe?ikym," ac'ój?am.

"Mortal people dying,
following upon death,
they will be laid longwise in the river;
and when they have lain there,
they will come to life again," ac'ój?am.

Awéten, bísc'oj?am.

Having done so, he remained silent,
ac'ój?am. (135)

Amýni, mymý béj?im, Wépam wewéjc'oj?am:

However, again, Coyote spoke to him:

"Wónodom, amýni ka?án wónomapem
amýni ka?án k'awím kanájdi támmapem,"
ac'ój?am.

"When people die, then they shall be dead
and then they shall be buried under the earth,"
ac'ój?am.

"Wónopem ma?át ka?án,
bének
ynójemenmapem," ac'ój?am.

"And when they are indeed dead,
the next day
they will not be going about again," ac'ój?am.

"Wónodom amýni, wónomak'an,"
ac'ój?am.

"When people die, they shall be dead,"
ac'ój?am.

"K'úldom amýni, k'úldom mamápem,"
ac'ój?am.

"When widowed, women shall be widows,"
ac'ój?am.

"Adóm kaʔán lólmapem,"
    ac'ójʔam.

"And then they shall cry in mourning,"
ac'ójʔam. (140)

"C'akám onódom,
    amýni kaʔán
c'akám onómapem," ac'ójʔam.

"Pine-pitch on their heads
and
pine-pitch on their faces," ac'ójʔam.

"Myjákkatim mapém
kak'án hiním béjby," ac'ójʔam.

"They will go about with it on their faces
and on their eyes also," ac'ójʔam.

"C'akáni kaʔán býmhelotodom, wákdom,
    jehéppintimapem," ac'ójʔam.

"Smearing themselves with pitch, groaning,
they will sound frightening," ac'ójʔam.

"Amám, maʔát, húkic'ikdom,
    c'ájim mádym púlidom,
amýni tetét jahát hybýkdom,
    jahát hybýkmapem," ac'ójʔam.

"But afterwards, indeed, forgetting,
marrying another man,
and so then feeling very happy,
they shall feel well again," ac'ójʔam.

"Jépsym kaʔán myjákkamapem,"
    ac'ójʔam.
"Sýttim májdym maʔát,
    sápyjnini maʔát,
pénenini maʔát kaʔán kúldom,
    c'áj kylékydom
        púlidom,
    amýni pí kylékydom,
tetét jahát hybýkmapem," ac'ójʔam.
"Kylém, béjby, pí kúldom,
    amét c'áj jépkylejledom,
    kaʔán jahámapem," ac'ójʔam.

"And husbands will do the same thing,"
ac'ójʔam. (145)
"A man, widowed for the first time,
for the second time,
even for the third time,
will marry another,
someone previously married,
and having married many times,
he will feel very well again," ac'ójʔam.
"A woman, too, many times bereaved,
still will take another husband
and all will be well," ac'ójʔam.

"Jepónim haʔáj jahá wéjejahak'an!"
    ac'ójʔam.
"Mí haʔáj, jepónim maʔát,
wónom mádyk'i jahát hybýkdom,
núkmape, wéjemenʔamkano," ac'ójʔam.

"A leader should really say what is good!"
ac'ójʔam.
"With you, leader,
mortal peoples' contentment and laughter,
you are not speaking for it," ac'ójʔam.

"Amét, haʔáj ní
wónom májdyk'i núkdom,

"On the contrary, it is I who speak
for mortal people's laughter,

Intaglio by Daniel Stolpe.

jahát hybýkdom,
ek'áwc'e?usmape wéjek'as,"
ac'ój?am.
"Kylóknono kíw," ac'ój?am.

contentment,
and delight in themselves,"
ac'ój?am. (150)
"Women too," ac'ój?am.

"Nenónopem májdym ma?át
béjdyk'ym kylé ojýpajdom
ka?án,
p'ýbcm májdym jákhybykmapem·
kylóknonom béjby majákkamapem ka?án,"
ac'ój?am.
"Níha?áj jepónim,
adóm tetét jahá wéjek'as!" ac'ój?am.
Ac'ój?am Wépam.

"Indeed an old man,
flirting and playing around with a young
woman, should
feel like a young man again;
and women should feel that way, too,"
ac'ój?am.
"I too am a leader,
and what I say is very good!" ac'ój?am.
Ac'ój?am Coyote.

Amýni, myjím, jepónim, wewéjmenwet,
bísc'oj?am:

Then he, the leader, said nothing,
but he thought to himself, ac'ój?am: (155)

"Mí ha?áj ypék'anbenini
ónk'ok'ojto?amkano,
amám, wéjemenwet,
wónokym k'ódom mabó," ac'ój?am.
Mym tetém májdym, húhejjeto, ka?áj
kac'ój?am.

"You, since you have
overcome me every time,
accordingly, without my saying so,
let there be death in the world," ac'ój?am.
This great man, thinking, did this,
kac'ój?am.

Ám kaním, wasása myk'í hésbobopajc'oj?am.
Ám kaním, ynódojc'oj?am.
Momím bódi, pénem c'ak'ác'ak'a
in?ántodi
jymýkitc'oj?am.
Ám kaním, ypínc'oj?am.

Finished, he got his things together, ac'ój?am.
Finished, he started off, ac'ój?am.
At the water's path, he set two scouring
rushes, one on
either side of it, ac'ój?am. (160)
Finished, he came away hitherwards,
ac'ój?am.

T'íkte ypínc'et,
myjím jahám p'ýbe myk'í,
wojómenkym ma?át:
"Momí hewínopi!" ac'ój?am.
Amýni hé?okitc'oj?am.

The other had only gone a little ways,
to that fine son of his,
whom he had never sent outside:
"Go and fetch some water!" ac'ój?am.
So then he went down to fetch some,
ac'ój?am.

Intaglio by Daniel Stolpe.

Amám ýtpinc'et, myjím c'ak'ác'ak'am
  sok'ótkypem húskym jákkadom,
    méhjodojim kaním,
    myjím té wónotic'oj?am.

As he went down, those rushes
took on the likeness of rattlesnakes,
and when they were finished biting him,
that child died, ac'ój?am.

    Amýni Wépam pelípc'oj?am:
"Béjbym ka?ájmenkym matási!"
      ac'ój?am.
    "Jewéj!" ac'ój?am.
  "Wónomenkym k'ódo matá!"
      ac'ój?am.
   "Té ník hónwe?ititibene?e!"
      ac'ój?am.
    "Jewéj! ac'ój?am.
Jahát ka?ájmenkym matás!" ac'ój?am.
  "Ypék'anbenini mínk'i wéje
    mín t'ikc'etas!"
      ac'ój?am.

So then Coyote cried out, ac'ój?am: (165)
"May I never say such things again!"
ac'ój?am.
"Come back!" ac'ój?am.
"Let there be no death in the world!"
ac'ój?am.
"You must make my son come back to life!"
ac'ój?am.
"Come back!" ac'ój?am. (170)
"I will never say such things again!" ac'ój?am.
"From now on I will always pay heed to
what you say!"
ac'ój?am.

    Héjpinc'oj?am
Myná ma?át, pínhej hej nomenwet,
    ypínc'oj?am.
    Bínmec'oj?am.
  Batápajmenc'onodom,
    sówwonoc 'oj?am.
    Ac'ét ypínc'oj?am.

He ran after him, ac'ój?am.
The other paid him no mind
but kept coming on hitherwards, ac'ój?am.
He pursued him, ac'ój?am.
Unable to overtake him,
he let him go, ac'ój?am. (175)
Meanwhile, the other continued on,
ac'ój?am.

"Wasám hap'á ní; tetét pín?inu
  ónk'ok'ojtosmyni,
    ník katídak'an,
    té wónotidadom,"
      ac'ój?am.
Án kaním, jesánoc'oj?am.

"I was bad: in return for the many times I
have won out over him,
he has done this to me,
killing the child,"
ac'ój?am.
It being finished, he stopped in his tracks,
ac'ój?am.

  "O! batápajmenmawet,
héjnomenmak'as," ac'ój?am.

"Oh! As I will never catch up with him,
I will chase him no longer," ac'ój?am. (180)

SEVEN

K'ódojapem Bom / Worldmaker's Trail

K'ódojapem Bom

"Amádi, mín wewéjbosdom:
'mín kaníwonom bíshukitmadom,'
kájk'as," ac'ój?am.
"Mí ka?ámkano kaním májdym,"
ac'ój?am.
"Amádi mín bíshukitweten,
jewéjdom, bísmak'as,"
ac'ój?am.

"Amám uním k'ódo jahámenmyni,
jadýkdykmak'as;
amám, jadýkdyk?is,
amám héki, púkma?amkano," ac'ój?am.

Worldmaker's Trail

"There, completing my speech for you:
'you shall dwell here all your life,'
I said," ac'ój?am.
"You shall be the last of my people,"
ac'ój?am.
"Now that I have told you to dwell here,
I shall depart and remain over there,"
ac'ój?am.

"If things are not just right in this country,
I shall make them so;
and when I have done that,
then later, you will be born," ac'ój?am.

Serigraph by Daniel Stolpe.

Ac'ét, ypínc'oj?am.	Meanwhile, he[1] came along this way, ac'ój?am.
Yjéwebisim, mydí, C'uc'újedi, amýni yc'ópinc'oj?am.	Continued traveling, to there, at Ch'uch'uje,[2] so then he came along this way, ac'ój?am.
Leléjc'opinc'oj?am.	He crossed over and along the slope, ac'ój?am.
Ac'ét, mac'ój?am.	Meanwhile, mac'ój?am.
Henánte k'umhým,	Down the slope was a sweathouse,
C'uc'újem Kylóknonok'i k'úk·mhým;	the house of the Pissing Women;
amánan, mac'ój?am	from thence, mac'ój?am,
májdy hénotic'oj?am.	they killed people all around, ac'ój?am.
Mym kylóknonom,	These women,
ypékanbeninim, májdym ýtnoc'et,	washing away everyone, killing people,
mynánmwónoti yjéc'oj?am.	They killed them as they passed by, ac'ój?am.
Amánan k'an, c'ec'ój?am.	And from thence, they saw him, ac'ój?am. (5)
Adóm k'an,	And then,
c'uc'úsitoc'oj?am.	they shot streams of piss across at him, ac'ój?am.
Jahát ypé,	He managed to get safely over the ridge,
myk'í tépkyni bit'íwkit	sticking his flint-flaker into the ground,
ysítopinc'oj?am.	he made it over, ac'ój?am. (10)
Ypék'ano	Getting over that way
ysítopindom,	until he was out of danger,
ysípc'oj?am.	he kept going along, ac'ój?am.
Ám kaním, ypínc'oj?am.	Having done that, he came along thither, ac'ój?am.
Ypinim kaním mydi P'ic'ádajtom týnkytok'i bíspedi, okítc'oj?am.	Coming at last to where the Mink and his little brother were living, he arrived there, ac'ój?am.
Ám kaním ujúkc'oj?am.	And finally he camped for the night, ac'ój?am.
Amýni myjím téc'om wéjec'oj?am.	So then those two youngsters spoke, ac'ój?am.
"T'újetitibene?e nisá," ac'ój?am.	"You should fix a trap for us," ac'ój?am. (15)
"Túj?asma, as hesíwet nisá julúmdawe oký?am," ac'ój?am.	"We have set traps, but something always breaks the trap," ac'ój?am.

Serigraph by Daniel Stolpe.

"Amám, nisá
t'újetitibeneʔe,"
ac'ójʔam.
Amýni k'an, ýnnom kaním,
t'újec'ojʔam.

"Therefore, you
would do better fixing the trap for
us," ac'ójʔam.
And then, having gone down,
he fixed the trap, ac'ójʔam.

Ám kaním k'an, t'újebosim kaním,
okítim kaním,
wéjec'ojʔam:

And when he had done so, finished fixing
the trap, and having returned,
he spoke to them, ac'ójʔam:

"C'ewéjmenpada,
mínc'em,"
ac'ójʔam.
"Wewéjmenwet, mínc'em
bínmedojpada,"
ac'ójʔam.
"Awéten, mínc'em,
amádiʔim hyt'í,
mahák'ojdom,
mahádiknoweten,
k'úmlajc'et,
óllolokdinan mínc'em
wydýmʔinnoweten,
weléjepada," ac'ójʔam.
"Ac'ét k'an, mymý,
hyt'í hídom,
hénomapem," ac'ójʔam.

"Do not speak,
you two, about what you've seen,"
ac'ójʔam. (20)
"Saying nothing, you two
must go after them,"
ac'ójʔam.
"Having done this, you two will,
grabbing up some of that grease there,
taking it with you,
having carried it there,
while they are sweating,
you two
having thrown it into the smoke hole,
then you must run back," ac'ójʔam.
"Meanwhile, they,
breathing in the smell of grease,
will suffocate," ac'ójʔam.

Mamýni k'án, "héw!" ac'ójʔam.

And the two of them: "all right!" ac'ójʔam.

Awéten, yk'ójc'ojʔam.

Having established this, he went away,
ac'ójʔam. (25)

Ac'ét, májc'om c'ekátoc'ojʔam.

Meanwhile, the two of them kept watch,
ac'ójʔam.

Bénekto, pokóm t'íkteʔin háhadojc'et,
paléʔojom weʔéc'ojʔam.

In the morning, just as the sun was rising,
a condor circled about, ac'ójʔam.

Amýni, myjím hojpajʔim wewéjc'ojʔam:

Then the younger brother spoke, ac'ójʔam:

Serigraph by Daniel Stolpe.

"Paléʔojom weʔék'an—   "There's a condor circling around—
t'únodi nisák'i wókyk'an!"   something must be caught in our trap!"
ac'ójʔam.   ac'ójʔam.

Awét bet'ékdojc'ojʔam.   Having established this, they ran to it,
                                     ac'ójʔam. (30)
Witýmʔinnoc'ojʔam.   They rushed down, ac'ójʔam.
Wilékk' ojjebisim welédiknoc'ojʔam. They kept running until they reached it,
                                     ac'ójʔam.
Epínim Kojódi, wytýwc'onomadom,   Toward the Sky Valley, it [the condor] was
                                     pulling it and had
béjdyk éswowodiknoc'et,   pulled the trapped animal halfway out
welédiknoc'ojʔam.   when the two reached it, ac'ójʔam.

Ám kaním,   Having done so,
bet'ékdiknom kaním,   having jumped up to where it was,
hukótoc'ojʔam.   they cut it [the trapped animal] in two,
                                     ac'ójʔam.
Amýnim búknakim mydýk'y   So then the tail-end the two
jac'éc'ojʔam.   managed to save for themselves, ac'ójʔam
Amýni lulúm nakím   And so the head-end
wyt'ýwc'oc'ojʔam.   was pulled up into the air, ac'ójʔam. (35)

Mínminim, lat'ínpindom,   Milk, dripping down,
látjepem májc'o sýnc'edonudom,   dripped upon the two as they looked up,
símdi lat'ínnojotic'ojʔam.   dripping into their mouths, ac'ójʔam.
Amám k'an, mínminik'i latt'áwonom,   Thereupon, where the milk had dropped,
mac'ójʔam, c'áwam bymídi.   mac'ójʔam, to their chins and breasts.
Awetén, nanádi mym   Where it had so done, upon their chests,
mac'ójʔam,   mac'ójʔam:
—"minik'i lat'áwonom"—.   —"it is where the milk had dropped"—

Awéten k'an, májc'om myjí, kulúnannac'et,
          mahák' ok'oj ʔam.
          Mahák' ojjebisim,
          myjím C'uc'újek'i
     újdi mahádiknoc'ojʔam.

And then, as it got along toward evening,
they took it with them, ac'ójʔam
Taking it with them,
they carried it to the Pissing
Women's house, ac'ójʔam. (40)

Kulúc'et, k'úmlajdom, myjim kylóknono,
     júkbodom, jépc'etikyc'ojʔam.

Those women were sweating, just at dark,
dancing, they were terrible to see! ac'ójʔam.

          Ac'ét k'an, myjím hyt'í
          wydýmʔinnoc'ojʔam.
          —ólloloknan—
Ám kaním k'an, májc'om weléjec'ojʔam.

Meanwhile, the two
flung the grease in, ac'ójʔam
—through the smokehole—
Their task completed, they ran away, ac'ójʔam.

          Ac'ét k'an, myjím hybóm, c'ódojdom,
               p'it'úpkitc'ojʔam.

Meanwhile, that sweathouse, catching fire,
burnt to the ground, ac'ójʔam.

Yjéwebisim, májc'om hybódi myc'ók'i
          okítweten,
          májc'om bísc'ojʔam.

Continually running, those two ran away to
their home,
and the two of them stayed there,
ac'ójʔam. (45)

          Ac'ét k'an, K'ódojapem,
               yk'ójjebisim,
          Nákam Kojódi,
K'ákk'am týnkytodi ydíknoc'ojʔam.
     Amádi k'an, ujúkc'ojʔam.

Meanwhile, Worldmaker,
traveling along, arrived in
Big Meadows,[3]
where the Crow brothers lived, ac'ójʔam.
And so he made camp there, ac'ójʔam.

          Amýni májc'o jʔam:
          "Nikʔúsum!
     Nisá c'ámmi t'óktitibeneʔe!
T'ókmuldom as nisá wasáweʔam," ac'ójʔam.

Then those two brothers said to him, ac'ójʔam:
"Our Elder brother!
You ought to sharpen our knives for us!
Having them dull is bad for us," ac'ójʔam.

Amýni k'an, májc'o t'óktitic'ojʔam.

So then, he sharpened both beaks for them,
ac'ójʔam.

          Awéten k'an,
          ujúkdom bísjat'an,
          ynóc'ojʔam.

Having done so,
after he had camped there for a while,
he went on, ac'ójʔam.

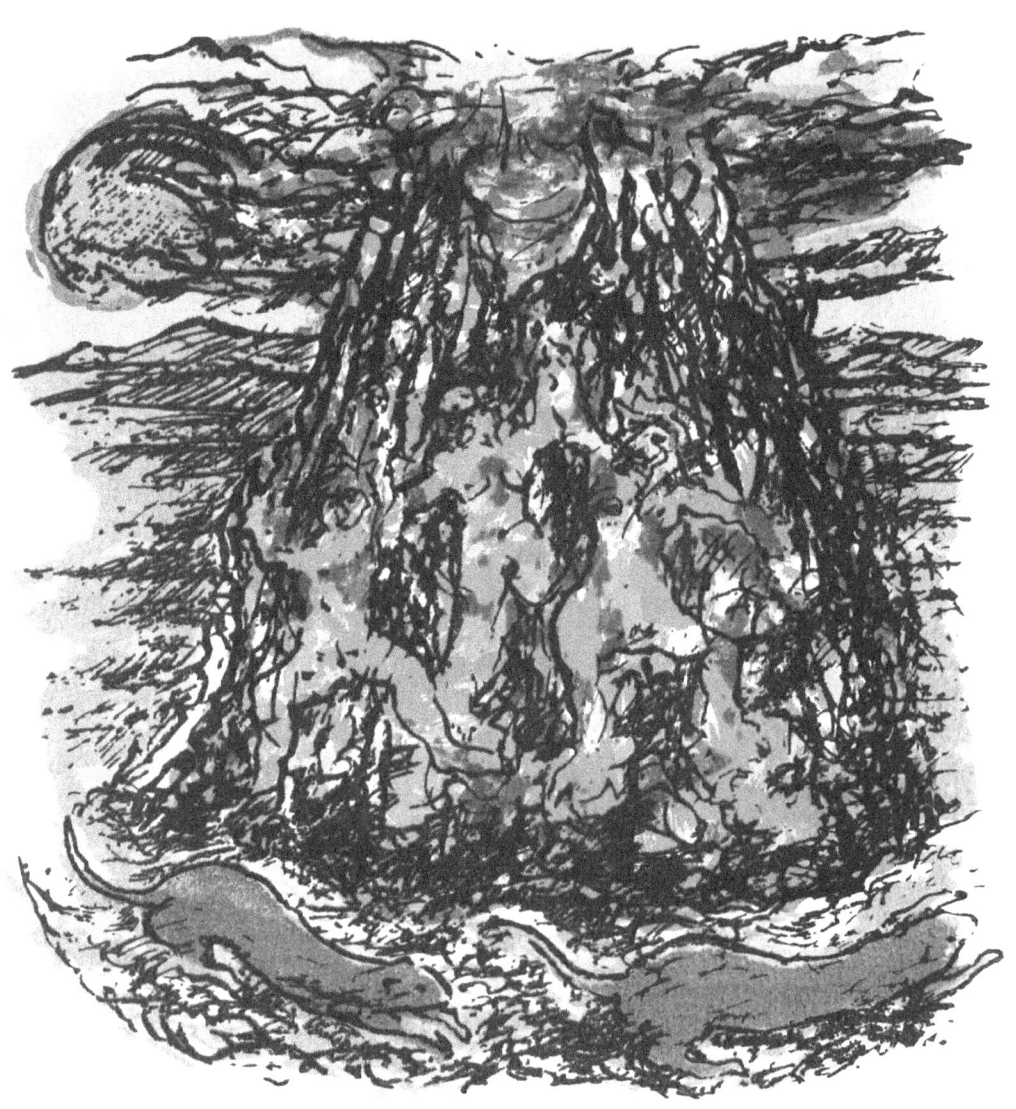

Serigraph by Daniel Stolpe.

Ynówebisim k'an,

As he kept on traveling,

Jákwik'elkym P'ýbec'om,

Two Boys Who Kill from a Canoe,

amác'ok'i sým,

a porcupine pet,

sýp'am sým,

living with them as a dog would,

t'ýjtanuc'oj?am.

was lying up on top of a rock, ac'ój?am.

Hesí ma?át

He was the kind

c'ewátajmenkym sým,

of dog who never failed to notice anything,

mac'ój?am.

mac'ój?am.

Amám ma?át k'an,

However,

c'eménc'oj?am.

he didn't see the one who was coming,

ac'ój?am.

Jedútwokitwetenk'an,
kak'ánajpin ypínweten,
jalálapdojim kaním.
dónim kaním,
wónotim kaním,
wac'ákydi myk'í jehéc'onom kaním,
ynóc'ojʔam.
—jedúdutkitim k'an—

He had dodged by lying flat on the ground,
and getting himself under the rock,
had reached up,
had grabbed it,
had killed it,
had tucked it into his belt,
and gone on, ac'ójʔam. (55)
—having dodged by lying down flat on the
ground—

Ac'ét k'an, májc'om
japájtowebiskyc'ojʔam.
Amám k'an májdyk k'ují
wyk'ýtc'onokym c'ámmi c'ebýkc'ojʔam.

Meanwhile, the two boys
kept on talking with each other, ac'ójʔam.
And then they were looking at the knife
they used for cutting off people's heads,
ac'ójʔam.

Májc'om, wéjedom:
"Maʔápeni ús kaʔúsaʔas,
wyk'ýtc'ono ʔyjédom wónom májdym k'ují!"
ac'ójʔam
—myc'ówet, japajtotodom—

The two were talking together:
"This is the kind of a thing we two always use
when we go around cutting off people's
heads!" ac'ójʔam
—thinking it was just the two of them—

Ac'ét k'an myjím
tetém májdym
hénmitnoc'ojʔam.
Am k'an bénmitnom kaním k'an,
sewínodo týst'ac'ojʔam.
Amýni k'an, c'ec'ójʔam.

But then that
great person
stepped down to where they were, ac'ójʔam.
And when he had gotten there,
he stood on the bank of the river, ac'ójʔam. (60)
And they saw him, ac'ójʔam.

Adóm k'an májc'om kylémam, k'abýkym
kyléc'yjc'ojʔam.
Myc'ó c'ec'ójʔam.

Then those two started to hide it,
but were too slow, ac'ójʔam.
He saw the two of them, ac'ójʔam.

"Ják mép ník mínc'emí," ac'ójʔam.
Amýni k'an májc'om
hasíppmc'ojʔam.
T'íktetesippinc'et,
c'ýjc'ojʔam.

"Hey, you two, bring me a boat!" he said.
And then the two
pushed him out of the water, ac'ójʔam.
But when they got it partway on the bank,
they stopped, ac'ójʔam.

Serigraph by Daniel Stolpe.

"T'íkne týpmitpin!" ac'ój?am.   "Jump on in from where you are," ac'ój?am.

Amýni k'an, ýtpinweten,   And then, climbing down the bank,
sewínodo týskitweten,   from the bank of the river,
bet'ékmitpinc 'oj?am.   he started to jump into the boat, ac'ój?am.
Befékmitpincom,   He started doing it,
bet'ékdapotoc'et,   but just as he was about to jump,
ka?áswosippmc'oj?am.   the two moved the boat, ac'ój?am.

Jak'á t'edísdojdom,
wodábo adóm matíc'oj?am.

Just so that he might slip, fall,
and then they could kill him, ac'ój?am.

Ypek'anbenini mac'ój?am.
Ka?át'ik amýni
mac'ój?am.
Wodáktemaldojdom, ac'ét,
mac'ój?am.
C'ámmini wódom,
k'ují wyk'ýtc'onokym;
amám junúkc'oj?am.

They attacked everyone that way, mac'ój?am. (70)
They would make it happen that way,
mac'ój?am.
People would slip and fall, and meanwhile,
mac'ój?am.
Striking them with their knives,
they would cut through their necks;
so they were crouched to spring on him,
ac'ój?am.[4]

Ac'ét, bet'ékdaweten, wéjec'oj?am.

But as he jumped aside, he spoke, ac'ój?am:

"Hénte!
Ník mínc'em mínc'ek'i c'ámmi c'ebýktipi!"
ac'ój?am.
"Hesátwet mínc'em
majákk'en jaháha c'ámmikypem?"
ac'ój?am.
Amýni týswojejat'an,
wihópdojc'oj?am.
Awéten, méjc'oj?am.

"Now then!
Let me have a look at your two knives!"
ac'ój?am. (75)
"Which of your two knives
appears to be better than the other?"
ac'ój?am.
Then the two stood up,
took out their knives, ac'ój?am.
Having done so, they gave them to him,
ac'ój?am.

Hápnomyni, méjdatoc'oj?am.

He took them and examined them at length,
ac'ój?am.

Ám kaním,
"Héw! Mínc'em jaháhalut'i
c'ámmikypem kaký?amkano!" ac'ój?am.
"Yk'ójdom ka?ás," ac'ój?am.
"Uním k'ódo, mínc'em mákkitpem
majákk'eno?"
ac'ój?am.
"Uním jamánmanto
mínc'em majákk'eno
mákkitpem?" ac'ój?am.
"Uním jamándi, hójjam,

When he finished,
"Well! You two certainly seem to
have very fine knives!" ac'ój?am. (80)
"I'm going now," ac'ój?am.
"This country, you two know your way
around in it, I suppose?"
ac'ój?am.
"These many mountains around here,
you must feel at
home in them all?" ac'ój?am.
"On this mountain here, in olden times,

Serigraph by Daniel Stolpe.

jáknan hasípdom,

utípaʔajk'an,"

ac'ójʔam.

"Jakúkitc'ojʔam," ac'ójʔam.

"Uním jamánmanto, k'ódom;

mómbudutc'onodom

paʔájk'an aʔúsan," ac'ójʔam.

Adóm myjím

c'ámmini héwwakatnojedom,

ypék'andykbem k'ódojna

héwwakatnojedom,

wéjec'ojʔam.

the people came out of a boat,

and left it there,"

ac'ójʔam.

"They abandoned the boat," ac'ójʔam. (85)

"These mountains around here, the lands;

before them,

deep waters had covered all," ac'ójʔam.

Then he took one of the knives,

pointing all around,

pointing toward each and every part of the

countryside,

he continued to speak, ac'ójʔam.

Ám kaním k'an,
myjím c'ámmini k'ují wódom,
wyk'ýtc'onoc'oj?am.
Ac'óko wónotic'oj?am.

Finally,
Striking them on the neck with that knife
he cut them through, ac'ój?am.
He killed them both, ac'ój?am.

Ám kaním, hadójnodom,
hasípc'oj?am.

Finishing that, putting them on his back,
he lifted them up out of the boat, ac'ój?am. (90)

Ac'ét, ót'okmam úcoj?am.

Sakým ínuc'oj?am.
Amádi, jymýkitc'oweten,
c'uc'úky wiláwsipc'oj?am.
Án kaním, mym májdyc'o
jydýmmitnoc'oj?am.
Let'á án kaním,
myjí let'ábosím kaním,
myjím c'uc'úkyni onýnkittidom,
k'énkittim kaním,
yk'ójc'oj?am.
Amák'an myjim mádyc'o jajónom
k'aní,
let'án kanim,
yk'ójc'oj?am.

Meanwhile, there was an earth oven nearby,
ac'ój?am.
A fire was burning in it, ac'ój?am.
And, laying the two down there,
he pulled off their pissers, ac'ój?am.
Having done this, he put the two bodies
into the oven, ac'ój?am.
When they had been covered up,
when they had been completely covered up,
bending their pissers over,
having finished laying the trap,
he went away, ac'ój?am. (95)
After he had done that with those two
persons,
when he had finished covering them over,
he went away, ac'ój?am.

Yk'ojc'oj?am—k'an—
Mujím májdyc'ok'i
mykótodi
ydíknoc'oj?am.—Kámjapdam Kylókbek'i
bíspedi—

He went away, ac'ój?am—and then—
He came to where the grandmother of the
two persons
lived, ac'ój?am.—to where Molting Woman
lived—

Awetén k'an myjím sýp'a wac'ákidi,
myk'í jehétdonupe
wydýmsitoc'oj?am.

And then he took the pet,
which was tucked under his belt and
flung it across at her, ac'ój?am.

"Sýp'a mý
lýtdom, pepí!" ac'ój?am.
—wydýmsitodom—

"Take that porcupine,
bake it in the ashes, and eat it!" ac'ój?am. (100)
—he threw it across—

Serigraph by Daniel Stolpe.

Ac'ét mykán jodýmsitopinc'oj?am.

  "Sýp'a mý lýtdom,

    pepí!"

  ac'ój?am.

 —k'an, jodýmsitodom—

But she threw it back at him, ac'ój?am.

"Take that porcupine, bake it in the ashes,

and eat it!"

ac'ój?am.

—and she threw it back across—

Ac'ét, béjbym méjwik'adojweten,
   béjbym jodýmsitoc'ojʔam.

But he, picking it up,
   threw it back again, ac'ójʔam.

   "Sýp'a
mý lýtdom, pepí!" ac'ójʔam.

"Take that porcupine,
   bake it in the ashes, and eat it!" ac'ójʔam.

Ac'ét, méjwik'adojdom mykán
   jodýmsitopinc'ojʔam.

But, she threw
   it back again, ac'ójʔam. (105)

"Lýtdom, pepi!" ac'ójʔam.

"Bake it and eat it!" ac'ójʔam.

Amýni, myjím májdym,
   sá héjjuwajweten,
   jymýttonoc'oj ʔam.

So then that man,
   spreading the embers apart,
   laid it down into them, ac'ójʔam.

Ám kaním, let'án kaním,
   kíwsusukitdom,
   tújc'ojaʔm.

Having done so, having covered it over,
   stretching out with his back to the fire,
   he went to sleep, ac'ójʔam.

Anám kíwsukinuc'ojʔam.

So he usually slept with his back to the fire,
ac'ójʔam.

Jamájim maʔát
   kajím makýc'ojʔam.
   —holókom kajím—

Indeed, it was only the appearance of his
self; in truth a log was there,
ac'ójʔam.—a rotten log— (110)

Amák'an, myjím kylókbem,
suné myk'í jymýʔasitom kanim,
   bátakinujat'an,
   wóc'ojʔam.
Ámkabyk'ym, júsasawajtatic'ojʔam.

Then that old woman reaching across,
having picked up her stone pestle,
   taking careful aim,
   bashing the log with it, ac'ójʔam.
She made it burst and fly all to pieces,
ac'ójʔam.

"Hám! hám!" ac'ójʔam.
"C'ájʔi as mín mý húpajdom, tapópak'asi!"
   ac'ójʔam.
"Jahát as tené hésmen tíkkasi!" ac'ójʔam.
Holókom kajím makýnoc'ojʔam.

"Well, well!" ac'ójʔam.
"I didn't think that was really you there,"
ac'ójʔam.
"It looked like some old thing!" ac'ójʔam.
The rotten log did look like him,
ac'ójʔam. (115)

Serigraph by Daniel Stolpe.

Mym
kíwsusukitim
hésmen yk'ójwonokyc'oj?am.

Ac'ét, ypém jamájim mawónom
kyc'ój?am.
Kíwsukinupem
jákkanudom,
ypém jamájim ma?át,
c'ájmen k'an, bet'éksipim kaním,
welék'ojc'oj?am.

He, who appeared
to be lying with his back to the fire,
had already gone away to some other place,
ac'ój?am.
Meanwhile, only a semblance
had remained, ac'ój?am.
Though seeming to be lying with his back to
the fire,
it was indeed only a semblance.
by and by, she jumped up and ran away,
ac'ój?am.

"Nikpejim téc'o, áj syʔýj,
hésmen pebóslewjakk'en!"
ac'ójʔam.
Welédiknodom, aʔájdom,
jynýswojdom,
k'abýk'ym k'éndi
diwóc'ojʔam.

"My two grandsons, I suppose
he must have long since eaten them!"
ac'ójʔam.
Talking to herself, running,
just as she was stooping down
to take the two out
she was caught in the trap, ac'ójʔam. (120)

Adóm k'an, ypék'anim májsem
hénoc'ojʔam.

And so he killed off all three of them,
ac'ójʔam.

Ac'ét k'an mým, maʔát ánwet,
yk'ójc'ojʔam.
Yk'ójjebisim k'an,
Hýkwom Kylókbek'i bíspedi,
ydíknoc'ojʔam.
Ám kaním k'an, mydí ujúkc'ojʔam.
ʌám kaním k'an, béjbym bének
ynódojc'ojʔam.

But he, paying no mind to that,
went his way, ac'ójʔam.
After he had traveled for a long time,
came to where Grouse Old Woman lived,
ac'ójʔam.
Having done so, he made camp there, ac'ójʔam.
Having done so, again
he went on in the morning, ac'ójʔam. (125)

Ynódojdom k'an, ynówebisim,
Pánom Kylókbek'i újdi
ydíknoc'ojʔam.

He set out and kept going along,
until he came to Grizzly Old Woman's house,
ac'ójʔam.

Amám k'an,
pénem téc'o wac'ák ʔidi myk'í jehétdojpe,
ydiknodom,
wy dýmsitoc'ojʔam.
"Sáwwali as mý mójjudom,
peʔúsan!"
ac'ójʔam.

When he got there,
he had her two children tucked under his belt,
reaching there,
he threw them across, ac'ójʔam.
"Singe the hair off these gray squirrels and
eat them!"
ac'ójʔam.

Ám kaním, c'ekínuc'et,
jok'ók'oskitim kaním kíwsusukitc'ojʔam.

Then, while she looked down at them,
he lay down with his back to the fire,
ac'ójʔam.

Ám kaním, hésmen yk'ójwet
mac'ójʔam,

But in fact, he had already gone away,
ac'ójʔam.

Serigraph by Daniel Stolpe.

Ypém jamájim maʔát
tújpemjákkanudom,
mac'ójʔam.

Only a semblance
looking like a sleeper was there, (130)
mac'ójʔam.

Amá k'an sýkky myk'í,
jymýdojim kaním,
jymýʔasitom kaním, bóc'ojʔam.
Ám k'abýk'ym, kají bócojʔam.

And then she,
having taken up her digging stick,
swung it around to hit him, ac'ójʔam.
But what she hit was a log, ac'ójʔam.

"Jahát as tené mín cájmeni min
húpajk'as!" ac'ójʔam.
"Ham, ham! Mítapom kaná
hónwejmaʔamkano?"
ac'ójʔam.
Awéten, bínmedojc'ojʔam.
Myk'í wosót'a wilílimmotoc'ojʔam.

"I was right when I thought you were
something different!" ac'ójʔam.
"Well, well! Did you think
you are going to live?"
ac'ójʔam. (135)
And she set out to find him, ac'ójʔam.
Whirling her skirt so that it fluttered about,
ac'ójʔam.

Amýni, k'ódom c'ódojc'oj?am.   Then the countryside caught fire, ac'ój?am.
Tetédyk'ym jákkadom,   Seeming to be everywhere,
bolákamoto?innodom,   sweeping over the land,
tetédyk'ym jákkac'oj?am.   it seemed to be everywhere, ac'ój?am.

Amýni kan, epínc'oj?am: And then, he asked, ac'ój?am:
"Mí mak'á hesákym?" ac'ój?am.   "How is it going with you?" ac'ój?am. (140)
— Momí —   — Water —

"Ní ka?ás pólpolkym," ac'ój?am.   "I'm boiling and bubbling," ac'ój?am.
"Ní ka?ás tetéɩ p'ilískym!"   "I'm becoming very hot!"

Amýni: And then:
"Mí mak'á hesákym?" ac'ój?am.   "How is it with you?" ac'ój?am.
— Óm májdy —   — Rock person —

"Ní ka?ás p'ilísdom,   "I'm getting hot.
léjwonini ma?át pópkym!" ac'ój?am.   From time to time I burst!" ac'ój?am.

Amýni,   And then:
"Mí adóm mak'á hesákym?" ac'ój?am.   "How is it with you?" ac'ój?am.
— C'ám májdy —   — Tree person —

"Ní ka?ás tetét c'ókym, tetét p'ilís?usasi!"   "I'm burning mightily, I'll stay very hot!"
ac'ój?am.   ac'ój?am. (145)

"Mí adóm mak'á hesákym?" ac'ój?am.   "And how is it with you?" ac'ój?am.
— Púm májdy —   — Milkweed person —

"Ní ka?ás, p'ijém p'ik'ójwono,   "I, when it has passed,
hójpajdi wodóm bís?as,"   shall be what is left behind still standing,"
ac'ój?am.   ac'ój?am.

Amýni k'an, amá éstodi lýkmitweten;   And so, crawling out flat in the middle of it,
bísc'oj?am.   he remained there, ac'ój?am.

P'ijéwebisim, k'ódom p'it'úpk'ojdom,   It kept on burning, the land having burned up,
k'ódom bukúkujkitc'et,   and when the land had cooled,

Serigraph by Daniel Stolpe.

pají wic'íkc'oj?am.

she was still following his tracks, ac'ój?am.

Pají wic'ímytydom, ymytymyni,
hésmenani jajtapada
hano?ono?koc'o?am.[5]

Following his tracks, going all around,
his tracks appeared
to have gone into the burnt area,
ac'ój?am. (150)

"Wonónkomako!" ac'ój?am.

"May he be the one who has died!" ac'ój?am.

Awéten, jewéjc'oj?am.
Ac'ét yk'ójc'oj?am.

Having done this, she gave up, ac'ój?am.
And so she went home, ac'ój?am.

Yk'ójjebisim, ypíndom,
bylélekdojc'ojʔam.

Traveling along, coming this way,
he climbed up to the top of a ridge, ac'ójʔam.

Ám kaním, "Héw! Sumúm,
áj syʔýj
wónom májdyk'i pekým údom;
amýni k'an wónom májdyk lýkdojdom,
hejúnpintidom,
sumú hyjémapem . . .
amám t'ésnonom týswilim
mamáʔamkano,"
ac'ójʔam.

Then: "Well! Sugar pine cones,
I am thinking that
these will be food for mortal people;
and so mortal people will be climbing up,
throwing down,
and gathering up the sugar pine cones . . .
therefore you're going to be short and
low-limbed,"
ac'ójʔam. (155)

Awéten, ypínc'ojʔam.

Having done so, he came on thither, ac'ójʔam.

Ac'ét k'an, wasópem,
Wépam májdym hójpaj
ʔyjéc'ojʔam.
Amám k'an, myjídi okítdom:
"Héw! Hesátimadom, ájte,
atí t'ésnopem c'á húkit
amám?" ac'ójʔam.
Ám kaním c'uc'úpajc'ojʔam.
"Wéh! Maʔántedojdi sumúm p'í lut'ím
okýk'an,
amápem kaʔán c'edónudom,
lýkdojc'yjdom,"
ac'ójʔam.

Meanwhile, in a bad mood,
Coyote person came
along after him, ac'ójʔam.
And thereupon, coming to that place:
"Well! Why, I wonder,
did he make this tree so
short?" ac'ójʔam.
And then he pissed on it, ac'ójʔam.
"Wéh! Now there are many sugar pine cones
high up,
and so when people see them,
they will have to climb up to them,"
ac'ójʔam. (160)

Awéten k'an, ypíncojʔam.

And having done so, he went on his way,
ac'ójʔam

Amám, mym, Kŏdojapem,
ypín kaním, bydójkinum;
c'enúmitc'ojʔam.

Now he, Worldmaker,
had come along this way for
a while; he sat down and took a look around,
ac'ójʔam.

Ám kaním, "Unídi mamák'an wónom
májdym majhí;

And then: "Here is where mortal
people will fish for salmon with nets;

Serigraph by Daniel Stolpe.

adóm húmindom, unídi jajókitdom
k'an wajómapem," ac'ój?am.
"Uc'án béjby
mý myjákkatim mapém," ac'ój?am.

Ám kaním, ynódom,
ynódojdom, ypínc'oj?am.
Mydí, Papádi,
papám piné myk'í bydójweten,
pec'ój?am.
Peját'an, cájmen tysk'adojim,
kaním,
c'enónuc'oj?am.

and so easily, here, stretching them out,
they shall throw them in," ac'ój?am.
"And on the other side,
they will do the same," ac'ój?am.

And then, setting out again,
traveling, he came this way, ac'ój?am. (165)
There, at the Place of the Little White Root,
he sat down and ate little white roots,
ac'ój?am.
And when he had eaten, he got to his feet,
then
he stood awhile and gazed southward,
ac'ój?am.

Ýnnoc'oj?am.

yk'ójjebisim, yk'ójjebisim,

Hanýlekem Kojódi ymítc'oj?am.

He started off downhill,

kept going, kept going

until he came to Honeylake Valley, ac'ój?am.

Adóm: "Héw! Jahám k'ódom unídi
okýk'as," ac'ój?am.

Then: "Well! I still have this good country
left," ac'ój?am.

"Wépam májdym k'ódo wíhjadom,
wasám k'ódo húkitc'et,
ní unídi nenópem májdyk'i tújc'enokym,
k'ódo húkitmak'as tené," ac'ój?am.
"Amádi k'an, wónom májdym,
nenópem májdym
mydí pijétodom
béjdyk?im májdym ma yjémak'an,"
ac'ój?am.

"While Coyote person is spoiling the world,
making it bad,
here I'll make a country where old people
may reawaken," ac'ój?am. (170)
"And thenceforth, mortal people,
old people,
they can bathe here
and come out young again,"
ac'ój?am.

Awéten k'an,
jamánbe hukítc'oj?am.
Támp'ip'itdiknodom k'an,
wodónuwebisc'oj?am.

Having said so,
he made a small mountain, ac'ój?am.
Standing up from the valley, sloping up
steeply, ac'ój?am.

"Unídi ka?án ydójjebisim, ydójjebisim,
wónodojwet ydíknomapem
nenópem májdym,"
ac'ój?am.
"Awéten k'an,
pijétodom,
béjdyk?immapem," ac'ój?am.
Awéten k'an, ykójc'oj?am.

"Here climbing, climbing,
until they get to the very
top, old people will get there almost dead,"
ac'ój?am.
"Having done this,
when they have bathed in this pool,
they will be young again," ac'ój?am.
This being done, he went away, ac'ój?am. (175)

Ykójc'oj?am.
Amám amánan ynódojdom,
ékdadojkydi
yc'ónoc'oj?am.

He went off, ac'ój?am.
Thereupon, setting out,
to where the sun comes up,
He crossed over, ac'ój?am.

Ac'ét k'an, myjím Wépam
ysítoc'oj?am.

And meanwhile that Coyote
was going about here and there, ac'ój?am.

Serigraph by Daniel Stolpe.

Yk'ójc'oj?am.
Amám k'an, myjím jamáni c'ec'ój?am.

He came across, ac'ój?am. (180)
And thereupon, he saw that small mountain, ac'ój?am.

"Unim, ájte, hesí adóm ejáti áman?"
ac'ój?am.
C'ebýkc'onoc'oj ?am.
C'edónuhanoj ec'oj ?am.
"C'uc'úpajmak'as kaná!" ac'ój?am.
Kojóm éstona,
c'epípitnoweten k'an,
c'uc'úpajc'oj?am.

"This hill, I wonder, why is it the way it is?"
ac'ój?am.
He looked it all over, ac'ój?am.
He stared at it for a while, ac'ój?am.
"I think I'll just piss on it!" ac'ój?am.
He took another quick look at the hill,
there in the middle of the valley,
and he pissed on it, ac'ój?am. (185)

Amýni k'an myjim jamánim kajdom, k'an
myjím kájwonodom, héjukitmyni,
myjím momím wasáminodom,
myjím paláwajkyk'i,
Ujdi Myjím Momí wadymmitc'oj?am.
Adóm k'an myjí
ypék'anudom,
opítkinuwebisc'oj?am.

Amám, mac'oj?am
"Húk'oj ypék'anudom," opítkinuc'oja?m.

And so then that mountain toppled over, and
when it had fallen, it broke open,
and that water spilled out,
into
the House of the Great Serpent, ac'oj?am.
And then the water kept filling up
everything
until it had filled up the whole valley,
ac'oj?am.
Thereupon, mac'oj?am:
"That lake still remains full, just the same,"
ac'oj?am.

"Wónom májdym amák'an ník:
'Óskypem Jamáni, Wépam, c'uc'úpajdom,
kájwonotipa?aje!'
adom k'an, núkdowejemapem,"
ac'oj?am.

"Mortal people, about me:
'Coyote pissed on Oskypem Mountain,
and made it tumble down!'
and then they will laugh and talk about it,"
ac'oj?am. (190)

"'Wépam ka?án myjím betéjmen, tetét
éptic'et,
K'ódojape ónk'ojdom,'"
wasótipac'oj?an.
Adóm k'an: "'Éptim ha?áj Wépam,
húkespem!'
atótodom ka?án
myséwet,
japájtotodom, núkmapem,"
ac'oj?am.

"'Coyote was the one, in ancient times, who,
getting the best of
Worldmaker,
making him angry,'" ac'oj?am.
"And then: 'How strong Coyote is,
how clever!'
that's what they'll recognize
among themselves
when they are talking together, laughing,"
ac'oj?am.

"Wépam as ka?úsas!"

"I will be Coyote forever!"

Wépam, awéten,
majákk'en
mym Óskypem Jamánim syhéjhejnonopem,
"Wówówówówówóweten!" welénoc'oj?am.

Coyote, having done this,
going along by the side of
where that Oskypem Mountain had been,
"Wowowowowoweten!" he ran crying out,
ac'oj?am.

"Amápem ka?án ník wónom májdym!"
ac'oj?am.

"Mortal people will talk about me!"
ac'oj?am.

Serigraph by Daniel Stolpe.

Yk'ójc'oj?am,	And he went away from there, ac'ój?am,
mynánbe.	went away.
Hesí ma?át húhejjemenwet, y'kójc'oj?am.	He was not thinking about anything at all, ac'oj?am.
—myk'í tawáli hap'á tawálbosweten—	—because all his work was done—
Kaním, ac'oj?am.	It is done, ac'ój?am. (195)

NOTES

1. This is K'ódojapem.
2. Also Ch'uch'uyaa, Soda Springs, and Soda Rock. See Shipley translation: "Pissing Place."
3. Ten years after Hanc'ibyjim told this story, Nakam Koyo was flooded for hydroelectric power and is now under Lake Almanor.
4. This story of a hero who transforms a deadly landscape into a place where human beings can live is widespread throughout the West. But the decapitation details in this version may also reflect recent settler history and the traffic in "Indian scalps" and "Indian heads" that had been prevalent in the nineteenth-century Susanville, Marysville, Honey Lake area, and funded by the California state treasury (Lindsay 2012).
5. This line is in Dixon and has been restored here. Unlike similar instances, the reconstruction after the first two words in Shipley's morphology and phonology is uncertain.

3

Pronunciation and Lessons

EIGHT

How to Pronounce Maidu

William Shipley

Like most languages in the world, Maidu had no writing system in the old days. In order to write things down in Maidu, it is necessary to make up an accurate system so that there will be a letter for each Maidu sound. We can use any letters at all for this as long as we know what sound each letter stands for. The easiest thing to do is to use letters from the alphabet we use for writing English, which is more or less the same alphabet used for writing French, Spanish, German, and many other languages. The alphabet we use for English was invented by the ancient Romans for writing Latin. That's why our alphabet is called the Latin alphabet.

You may already know that when we use the Latin alphabet to write Spanish, the letters are used for somewhat different sounds than they are when we write English. The sounds of each language in the world are different from the sounds of any other language, and this is true of Maidu. If you want to learn to pronounce Maidu correctly, you have to learn what each letter of the Maidu alphabet sounds like. This is easy in a way, because every letter in the Maidu alphabet is pronounced consistently.

The hard part is learning the Maidu sounds. Some are more or less like English, but some are different. There are six vowels and fourteen consonants. The Maidu alphabet does not contain *f, g, q, r, v, x,* or *z.* The reason these letters are not used is that the sounds they usually stand for are not in Maidu. But remember that some other letters—the ones we will use to write Maidu—are not pronounced as they are in English, or French, or Spanish, or any other language except Maidu.

Let's talk about the six vowels first. Five sound pretty much like some vowels sounds in English.

a always sounds like "a" in "father." Example: mám 'hand'.

e always sounds like "e" in "met." Example: wé 'vomit'.

i always sounds like "ee" in "keep." Example: mí 'you'.

o always sounds like "aw" in "law." Example: lóm 'wild goose'.

u always sounds like "oo" in "moon." Example: mú 'shoot'.

The little marks over the vowels are called *stress marks*. They simply mean that the vowel they are on is pronounced louder and stronger than other vowels.

There is a sixth vowel in Maidu, and it is not pronounced like any vowel in English. So we will write this vowel with a *y*. So you must remember that in Maidu the letter *y* does not stand for the same sound that it does in English! Here are some examples:

mymým	'that one'
nýwynto	'rock back and forth'
lylým	'star'

In these words, the vowel with the stress mark is louder and stronger than the other vowel. This *y* is pronounced by closing your teeth together, spreading your lips, and making a sound like people make when they step barefooted on a slug or a caterpillar. It will help if you can find someone who knows how to pronounce these Maidu words for you. If you want your Maidu to sound right, it's very important that you learn how to pronounce this vowel.

Now let's talk about the fourteen Maidu consonants. You know five of them already because they are in the examples for vowels that I've already given you: *l, m, n, t,* and *w.* They are pronounced much as they are in English. There are three more consonants that are also spelled and pronounced like English: *h, k,* and *p.*

hakáka	'bitter'
kylém	'woman'
pénem	'two'

So eight of the Maidu consonants are more or less like English. There is one more consonant that sounds like English but is spelled with a different letter. That is the consonant *j*, which is pronounced exactly like English *y.* If we're going to use the letter *y* for the strange Maidu vowel, then we have to use something else for the sound of *y.* The letter *j* is it.

jám 'cloud' (pronounced yam)	jóm 'flower' (pronounced yom)
jém 'feather' (pronounced yem)	jú 'rub' (pronounced yu)

That leaves us with five consonants that are not pronounced like anything in English, so we have to look at them one by one and see how they are made.

Maidu *b* is made by forming a little vacuum or suction inside your mouth before you pull your lips apart, suck the air out of your mouth with your lips closed, <u>then</u> make the *b*. This is easy to do but hard to describe clearly. If you can, find someone who can make this sound for you. Maidu *d* is made the same way, making a vacuum behind your tongue before you pull it down to make the *d* sound. Make an English *d* first, so that you'll see what you're doing with your tongue. Here are some examples to practice on:

bám	'salt'	dáldalpe	'white'
bonóm	'ear'	dúpe	'cold'
béjby	'again'	didíkim	'gnat'

The Maidu letter *c* can be pronounced in two ways. Some speakers used to say "ts" as at the end of the word *hats*. Other speakers used to say "ch" as in *church*. You can pronounce this consonant either way, but it would be good to stick to one way or the other. Practice on these words:

catáta	'rattle'	cykýcyky	'tickle'

Maidu *s* is quite different from English *s*. When it is followed by a vowel, it is pronounced by pulling your tongue back into your palate so that it sounds "harsher" than an English *s*. Again, it's easy to do if you can hear it, though very hard to describe. When the Maidu *s* is not followed by a vowel, it is hissed more strongly than in English. Practice on these examples:

síwsiwpe	'black'	wásweje	'curse'
wasá	'bad'	hebáskym	'broom'

The last consonant is called a *glottal catch*. People make this sound when they're speaking English, but there's no way to spell it. One way to say "no" in English is to say something like "unh unh." If you'll do this, you'll hear that you close up your throat just before each syllable. Also, in English when you're warning a small child not to do something, you can say, "Ah ah! Don't do that!" Can you feel and hear that catch in your throat? That's just like the glottal catch in Maidu, and it is written with a single quotation mark when it occurs after a consonant. Where the glottal catch occurs between vowels, it can be written as ʔ. Here are some examples:

wiʔí	'to lack'	wajʔóm	'skunk'
maʔá	'to accomplish'	jéʔokit	'to invite to come'

The hardest thing to pronounce in Maidu is a combination of the glottal catch immediately after p, t, c, or k. Take the word "tree" as an example. The Maidu word is c'ám. (Remember that c sounds like "ch" or "ts.") You can practice by saying something like ca'ám and then trying to leave out the first a. Ca'ám, c'ám. Ca'ám, c'ám. Here are some more examples for practice:

p'op'om: po'opo'om, p'op'om (take out the first o) 'hay'
t'úm: tu'um, t'úm (take out the first u) 'fence'
k'an: ka'an, k'an (take out the first a) 'and'

This is very hard to get right, partly because in proper Maidu speech this combination of *p, t, c,* or *k* and glottal catch should be pronounced gently. You'll have to pronounce it strongly at first so as to get it right, then make it softer.

Here is the Maidu alphabet. If you've read this section carefully, you should know how each letter is pronounced.

a	h	m	t
b	i	n	u
c	j	o	w
d	k	p	y
e	l	s	' (glottal catch), ʔ between vowels

You must also write the stress mark, or you won't know which vowels to pronounce louder than others.

NINE

Reading the Maidu Language

Nine Beginning Lessons

William Shipley

LESSON 1

wépam	'coyote'	uním	'this, these'
mýdem	'brown bear'	aním	'that (over there) those'
hawím	'gray fox'	kak'án	'he, she, it is; they are'

Can you read this?

Wépam. Uním mýdem. Aním hawím. Uním kak'án wépam. Aním kak'án mýdem. Uním kak'án mýdem.

How would you say the following in Maidu?

That coyote.   That is a gray fox.

This is a brown bear.   This coyote.

Notice that there are no words for *the* or *a* or *an* in Maidu: Aním kak'án wépam. This means: There is the Coyote. Or it means: There is a coyote.

LESSON 2

májdym	'man; person'	unídi	'here'
kylém	'woman'	anídi	'there'
kylóknonom	'women'	hybódi	'in this house'

Can you read this?

Mýdem kak'án unídi. Kylóknonom kak'án hybódi. Májdym kak'án anídi. Uním kak'án kylém. Aním kak'án kylóknonom. Hawím kak'án unídi. Wépam kak'án anídi. Uním kak'án májdym. Aním májdym kak'án hybódi.

How would you say the following in Maidu?

These are the women.   The man is in the house.
That is a woman.   A man is in the house.
The coyote is in the house.   This is a gray fox.
A brown bear is here.   Those women are in the house.

LESSON 3

ní	'I'	k'umúdi	'in the roundhouse'
mí	'you'	jamándi	'on the mountain'
kak'ás	'I am'	séwdi	'in the river'
ka'ámkano	'you are'	kájdi	'on a log'

Since you can always tell the subject of a sentence from the ending on the words for *am*, *are*, and *is* in Maidu, you don't have to say the words for *I* (ní) or *you* (mí) unless you want to emphasize them. Look at these forms:

kak'ás	'I am'	ní kak'ás	'I am'
ka ámkano	'you are'	mí ka'ámkano	'you are'

You can always say the *ní* and the *mí* if you want to, but you don't have to. This is true for all verbs in Maidu. Notice that if you put *di* on the end of a word, it means 'in' or 'on,' depending on what makes sense. Also, k'umúdi means 'in <u>a</u> roundhouse' as well as 'in <u>the</u> roundhouse', and so forth.

Can you read this?

Ní kak'ás k'umúdi. Ka' ámkano jamándi. Uním májdym kak'án hybódi. Aním wépam kak'án kájdi. Kak'as unídi. Uním mýdem kak'án séwdi. Mí ka'ámkano kylém. Ní kak'as májdym.

How would you say the following in Maidu?

That gray fox is in the river. The brown bear is on the log. I am a man. The women are in the roundhouse. The coyote is on the mountain. You are in the house.

NOTE: An *m* that comes just before a *k* is pronounced like the *ng* in English *sing*. For example, ka' ámkano 'you are' is pronounced "ka' ángkano." Be sure to do this. We'll see why this is so when we have learned more Maidu.

LESSON 4

c'ek'ás	'I see'	pek'ás	'I eat'
c'e'ámkano	'you see'	pe'ámkano	'you eat'
c'ek'án	'he, she, it sees; they see'	pek'án	'he, she, it eats; they eat'

In English, there are sentences like these:

"I see him." "He sees me." "You see her." "She sees you."

Notice that when you're saying who does the seeing in English, you use *I*, *he*, and *she*, but when you're saying who is seen, you use *me*, *him*, and *her*. Something like that happens in Maidu, too, but in Maidu it's much more important. In Maidu, whatever or whoever does what the verb says—whoever sees or hears or carries, for example—has to have an *m* on the end of the word. You've already seen this:

Wépa͟m kak'án unídi.	A coyote is here.
Májdy͟m kak'án k'umúdi.	The man is in the roundhouse.
Kylóknono͟m kak'án jamándi.	Women are on the mountain.

The way we can talk about this is to call words like those in these sentences *subjects of the verb*. In Maidu, subjects of the verb—words that tell us who or what is doing what the verb says—always have an *m* on the end. Notice that this is not true of ní and mí. They are the only exceptions in the language. Maidu nouns with *m* on them are like the English pronouns *I*, *he*, and *she*. They are *subjects*.

Look at these sentences:

Májdym mýde cek'án.	The man sees the brown bear.
Kylóknono c'ek'ás.	I see the women.
Wépa͟m hawí c'ek'án.	The coyote sees the gray fox.
Hawím wépa c'ek'án.	The gray fox sees the coyote.

LESSON 5

Now we will talk about those four sentences at the end of the last lesson. Notice that the subject noun of each sentence has an *m* on the end of it. For example, in

Májdym mýde c'ek'án,

it is the person who is doing the looking and the bear that he is observing. So the word for "person"—májdym—has an *m* on the end. Now you may notice that the brown bear is what he's seeing—the brown bear is <u>not</u> doing the looking but is the *object* of the looking, what the person is seeing. Since mýde is the object of the verb, it does not have an *m* on the end. Any noun that is the subject of a verb in Maidu will have an *m* on the end. Any noun that is the object of the verb will not have an *m* on it. Let's look again at the last two sentences at the end of the fourth lesson:

| Wépam hawí c'ek'án. | The coyote sees the gray fox. |
| Hawím wépa c'ek'án. | The gray fox sees the coyote. |

In Maidu it is completely clear who is seeing and who is seen. Sometimes there's no word in a sentence to tell us who is doing what the verb says. In the second sentence at the end of the last lesson,

Kylóknono c'ek'án.   I see the women.

the verb itself lets you know who is doing the seeing—c'ek'ás can only mean "I see"—so that sentences like this one have an object noun but no subject noun, since the subject is expressed in the form of the verb.

Maidu is very different from English in another way. In English the subject comes first, then the verb, then the object. Example: "The man (subject) sees (verb) the brown bear (object)." In Maidu, the subject comes first, then the object, then the verb, that is, Maidu verbs are at the end of the sentence. Example: Májdym (subject) mýde (object) c'ek'án (verb). If you look back at the first three lessons, you will see that this is not true for the verbs that mean "am" (kak'ás), "are" (ka'ámkano), or "is" (kak'án). This is the only verb that may come before the object; actually, with this verb you have a choice. The two sentences below have exactly the same meaning and are both correct:

| Uním mýdem kak'án séwdi. | This bear is in the river. |
| Uním mýdem séwdi kak'án. | This bear is in the river. |

LESSON 6

In the second and third lessons, we had the following words:

hybódi	'in this house'	k'umúdi	'in the roundhouse'
jamándi	'on the mountain'	séwdi	'in the river'
kájdi	'on a log'		

Now you can see that these words all have *di* on the end of them and that they all tell the location of something. When you're talking about live creatures, this *di* means something like "where the ___ is."

májdydi	'where the man is'
kylóknonodi	'where the women are'
mýdedi	'where the brown bear is'
wépadi	'where the coyote is'

Nouns like all of these that tell the location of something we will call *locative* nouns. There is something special to know about how to make these locative nouns. If the object form of the noun ends in *i*, then you drop the *i* before you attach the locative *di*. So, for example, "gray fox" has these different forms:

Subject	Object	Locative
hawím	hawí	háwdi

Notice that the stress changes, too, when you do this. Here are all the nouns we've had so far, with the three forms we've learned about. See if you can guess what each of these words means:

Subject	Object	Locative
wépam	wépa	wépadi
mýdem	mýde	mýdedi
hawím	hawí	háwdi
májdym	májdy	májdydi
kylém	kylé	kylédi
kylóknonom	kylóknono	kylóknonodi
hybóm	hybó	hybódi
k'umúm	k'umú	k'umúdi
jamánim	jamáni	jamándi
sewím	sewí	séwdi
kajím	kají	kájdi

LESSON 7

Can you read this?

> Wépam myk'í hybódi bísk'an. Mýdem ydíknok'an. Wépakí hybó cék'án.
> "Hesásak'a?" ak'án mýdem.
> "Jahák'as. Mínk'i k'ódojdi hesásak'ade?" ak'án wépam.
> "Ní béjby as jahák'as," ak'án mýdem.
> Mýdem yk'ójk'an. Wépam bísk'an.

New words

bís	'be in a place, stay, live'	ydíkno	'arrive'
myk'í	'his, her, its'	wépak'i	'coyote's'
a	'say'	hesásak'a	'how are you?'
jahá	'good, be good, be well'	mínk'i	'your'
k'ódom	'country, place, land'	hesásak'ade	'how is it?'
k'ódojdi	'in the place, in the country'	béjby	'also'
yk'ój	'go, go away' as (emphasizes *ni* at beginning of sentence)		

mínk'i k'ódojdi hesásak'ade? 'How is everything at your place?'

Notice that the verbs in this list are given without any endings. That's because the endings are always the same. Let's see what we have so far, looking back over the earlier lessons:

kak'ás	'I am'	ka'ámkano	'you are'	kak'án	'he, she, it is; they are'
c'ek'ás	'I see'	c'e'ámkano	'you see'	c'ek'án	'he, she, it sees; they see'
pek'ás	'I eat'	pe'ámkano	'you eat'	pek'án	'he, she, it eats; they eat'

Now let's add the new verbs that turn up in this lesson:

bísk'an	'he, she, it lives; they live'
ydíknok'an	'he, etc. arrives'
jahák'as	'I am well'
ak'án	'he, etc. says'
yk'ójk'an	'he, etc. goes away'

Note that the same endings are on all these verbs. We'll talk about this in the next lesson.

LESSON 8

We have to learn something about how to talk about verbs. When a verb has *I* as the subject, it is called first person. When the verb has *you* as the subject, it is called second person. When a verb has *he, she, it* or *they* as the subject, it is called third person. In Maidu, these three persons have different forms, as you can see from the list at the end of the last lesson. They are as follows:

First person: *kʼas*
Second person: *ʼamkano*
Third person: *kʼan*

These endings are the same for <u>all</u> verbs in Maidu, so all you have to know about a new verb that you've never seen or heard before is what the front part means without the ending. For example, when you find out that the verb for "talk" is wéje, then you know that "I talk" will be wéjekʼas, "you talk" will be wéjeʼamkano, and "he talks" (or "she talks" or "they talk") will be wéjekʼan. This part of the verb without the ending is called the *stem*. All you need to know is what the stem of any verb is, and you can put the right endings on.

It's clear that the Maidu third person, *kʼan*, can be talking about one person or more than one—it can mean "he," "she," "it," or "they." The same thing is true of the second person. It can mean "one of you" or "any number of you." But that's not so of the first person *kʼas*. It means only "I" and not "we." Maidu has three first person endings—one that means "I"—the one you already know, *kʼas*—another one that means "we two," and a third one that means "we three or more."

Here's an example of all these with the verb wéje:

1 SINGULAR	wéjekʼas	'I talk'	
1 DUAL (two)	wéjeʼamkʼas	'we two talk'	(-angkʼas)
1 PLURAL	wéjeʼemkʼes	'we three or more talk'	(-engkʼes)
2	wéjeʼamkano	'you one or more talk'	(-angkano)
3	wéjekʼan	'he, she, it talks; they talk'	

Note that all the verbs we've looked at so far are talking about what's going on right now. They're called *present verbs* or *present tense verbs*. When you talk about the past or the future in Maidu, you have to use other verb endings, as we'll see later on.

LESSON 9

Can you read this?

Hawím hybódi bísk'an.   Hawík'i hybóm kojódi kak'án.
Pánom ómk'ùmdi bísk'an.   Pánok'i ómk'umìm kak'án.
Mómpànom pakándi bísk'an.   Mómpànok'i pakánim c'ámk'òdodi kak'án.
Nisém k'umúdi bís'emk'es.   Nisék'i k'umúm unídi kak'án.
C'ámk'òdom kak'án jamándi.   Kojóm kak'án anídi. Nisám ka'ámk'as
                                              hybódi.

New Words:

kojóm	'valley, meadow'	pánom	'grizzly bear'
ómk'umìm	'cave'	mómpànom	'otter'
pakánim	'pool of water'	c'ámk'òdom	'forest'
nisém	'we (three or more)'	nisám	'we (two)'

In English, when we want to show that a noun is the owner of something, we use this: "The man's house," that is, "the house that belongs to the man." In Maidu, to show that a noun is the owner of something, we put on the ending *k'i*. To say "the man's house" in Maidu, we must say, "Májdyk'i hybóm."

This shows that the man possesses the house. We call *–k'i* the *possessive* ending. Now we have four possible forms for every Maidu noun.

Subject: mómpànom	'otter' (when it is the subject of the verb)
Object: mómpàno	'otter' (when it is the object of the verb)
Possessive: mómpànok'i	'otter's, of the otter'
Locative: mómpànodi	'where the otter is; the otter's place'

Note that c'ám is the word for "tree" and k'óódom is the word for "land, place, country," so that c'ámk'òdom, "forest," is really "tree place" or "tree country." Similarly, óm is "rock" and k'umim is "hole," so that ómk'umìm is really "rock hole." Also, momím is "water," so that mómpànom is really "water grizzly."

In this lesson there are some backward stress marks ('). The vowels marked like that are stressed some, but not as much as the main stresses.

APPENDIX: Place Names and Character Names in the Stories

NAME	GLOSS / TRANSLATIONAL COUNTERPART	LOCATION IN STORIES
Bám	salt	Chapter 6, lines 46, 82, 85, 87, 89
Beléwdi	at the side [of it], North	Chapter 4, lines 52, 108, 120, 127; Chapter 5, line 22
Cä́m	tree	Chapter 7, line 144
Cä́ndi	at the edge [of here], Northwest	Chapter 4, lines 51, 107, 119, 127; Chapter 5, line 16
C'iwíspólotkym	One Who Sticks a Mantle On, Robin	Chapter 4, lines 76, 97, 236
C'iwlutcónokym	One Who Throws Over to the Other Side, Robin	Chapter 4, lines 55, 79
C'ucújedi	Pissing Place, Chu'chu'ya Soda Rock	Chapter 7, line 2
C'ucújem Kylóknonoki	Pissing Women	Chapter 7, lines 5, 40
Ékdadojkydi	where the dawn rises, East	Chapter 4, lines 48, 105, 116, 127; Chapter 5, line 21
Epínim Kojó	Sky Valley, open sky	Chapter 4, line 5; Chapter 7, line 32
Hanýlekem Kojó	He Carries It Over, Honeylake Valley	Chapter 7, line 168
Hemém	gopher	Chapter 5, lines 125, 140, 195
Hýkwom Kylókbek'i	Grouse Old Woman	Chapter 7, line 123
Jákwik'elkym Pýbecóm	Two Boys Who Kill from a Canoe	Chapter 7, line 52
Jakúkim Jamándi	Canoe Mountain	Chapter 4, line 252
K'ákk'am	crow	Chapter 7, line 46
Kámjapdam Kylókbek'i	Moulting Woman	Chapter 7, line 98
Kokók'i kyćónokydi	Where it sets/goes down, West	Chapter 4, lines 50, 106, 118, 127; Chapter 5, lines 21, 76
Komódi	Where it goes across, South	Chapter 4, lines 49, 106, 117, 125; Chapter 5, line 22
K'ódom Éstodi	Middle of the World	Chapter 4, lines 163, 170, 235, 240; Chapter 5, line 91

K'ódojapem	Worldmaker	Chapter 4, lines 1, 28, 66, 69, 99, 240; Chapter 7, lines 46, 162, 191
Mákmakkym	Pilieated woodpecker	Chapter 5, line 177
Momí	water	Chapter 7, line 141
Nákam Kojó	Big Meadows, now Lake Almanor	Chapter 7, line 46
Óm	rock	Chapter 7, line 143
Óskypem Jamáni	Óskypem Mountain	Chapter 7, lines 190, 193
Palé'ojom	condor	Chapter 7, line 29
Papádi	Place of the Little White Root	Chapter 7, line 166
Pánom Kylókbek'i	Grizzly Old Woman	Chapter 7, line 125
Púm	milkweed	Chapter 7, line 146
P'ic'ádajtom	mink	Chapter 7, line 12
Pop'om	dry grass	Chapter 5, lines 130, 136
Sáwwali	grey squirrel	Chapter 7, line 128
Sumúm	sugar pine cones	Chapter 7, lines 155, 160
Sýp'a	porcupine	Chapter 7, lines 52, 100, 101, 104
Ujdi Myjím Momí	Hut of the Water Serpent	Chapter 7, line 186
Wépam	Coyote	Chapter 4, lines 22, 59, 71, 80, 93, 219; Chapter 5, lines 3, 52, 74, 123, 217, 239, 244, 256, 259, 263, 275, 285; Part 3, lines 17, 24, 26, 27, 39, 69, 79, 82, 84, 85, 97, 101, 108, 121, 128, 130, 132, 136, 154, 165; Chapter 7, lines 157, 170, 179, 190, 191, 192, 193

Note: All words repronounced by Maym Gallagher and transliterated by William Shipley.

BIBLIOGRAPHY

An Act to Provide for the Allotment of Lands in Severalty to Indians on the Various
    Reservations (General Allotment Act or Dawes Act), Statutes at Large 24, 388–91,
    NADP Document A1887. Access full transcript at www.ourdocuments.gov/doc
    .php?doc=50.

Anderson, Karen Lahaie. 2014. *Mountain Maidu Grammar.* Self-published.

Bakhtin, Mikhail. 1986. *Speech Genres and Other Late Essays.* Translated by Vern W.
    McGee. Edited by Caryl Emerson and Michael Holquist. Austin: University of
    Texas Press.

Basso, Keith. 1996. *Wisdom Sits in Places: Landscape and Language among the
    Western Apache.* Tucson: University of Arizona Press.

Bauer, William J., Jr. 2012. *We Were All Like Migrant Workers Here: Work, Community,
    and Memory on California's Round Valley Reservation, 1850–1941.* Chapel Hill:
    University of North Carolina Press.

Bauman, Richard, and Charles Briggs. 2003. *Voices of Modernity: Language Ideologies
    and the Politics of Inequality.* New York: Cambridge University Press.

Bibby, Brian. 2004. *Deeper than Gold: A Guide to Indian Life in the Sierra Foothills.*
    Berkeley: Heyday.

Brooks, Lisa. 2008. *The Common Pot: The Recovery of Native Space in the Northeast.*
    Minneapolis: University of Minnesota Press.

Brown, William Adams. 1910. *Morris Ketchum Jesup: A Character Sketch.* New York:
    Charles Scribner's Sons.

Cadena, Marisol de la. 2015. *Earth Beings: Ecologies of Practice across Andean Worlds.*
    Durham: Duke University Press.

Collins, James. 1998. *Understanding Tolowa Histories: Western Hegemonies and Native
    American Responses.* New York: Routledge.

Darnell, Regna. 1990. "Franz Boas, Edward Sapir, and the Americanist Text Tradition."
    Historiographia Linguistica 17 (1–2): 129–44.

Dixon, Ronald B. 1900a. "The Language of the Maidu Indians of California." PhD diss.,
    Harvard University.

———. 1900b. "Some Coyote Stories from the Maidu Indians of California." *Journal
    of American Folklore* 13: 267–70.

———. 1900c. "Basketry Designs of the Maidu Indians of California." *American
    Anthropologist* 2: 266–76.

———. 1902. *Maidu Myths.* Huntington California Expedition. *Bulletin, American
    Museum of Natural History* 17: 33–118.

———. 1903. "System and Sequence in Maidu Mythology." *Journal of American
    Folklore* 16 (60): 32–36.

———. 1905. *The Northern Maidu.* Huntington California Expedition. *Bulletin,
    American Museum of Natural History* 17: 119–346. New York: Knickerbocker
    Press.

———. 1911. "Maidu." In *Handbook of American Indian Languages*, 1:679–734. Bureau of American Ethnology, Bulletin 40. Washington DC: Government Printing Office.

———. 1912. *Maidu Texts*. Leyden, Netherlands: E. J. Brill.

———. 1931. "The Creation according to the Maidu." In *Source Book in Anthropology*, 2nd ed., ed. A. L. Kroeber and T. T. Waterman, 458–63. New York: Harcourt, Brace.

Du Bois, Cora. 1939. *The 1870 Ghost Dance*. Berkeley: University of California Press.

Dunbar-Ortiz, Roxanne. 2014. *An Indigenous Peoples' History of the United States*. Boston: Beacon Press.

Eargle, Dolan H., Jr. 2007. *Native California: An Introductory Guide to the Original People from Earliest to Modern Times*. San Francisco: Trees Company Press.

Errington, Joseph. 2008. *Linguistics in a Colonial World: A Story of Language, Meaning, and Power*. Malden: Blackwell.

Goldberg-Ambrose, Carole, and Duane Champagne, with assistance from Wallace T. Cleaves, Leroy Seidel, Chad Gordan, Patty Ferguson, Kit Winter, Lola Worthington, and Lori Soghomonian. 1996. "A Second Century of Dishonor: Federal Inequities and California Tribes." Sacramento: Advisory Council for California Indian Policy.

Golla, Victor. 2011. *California Indian Languages*. Berkeley: University of California Press.

Gruber, Jacob. 1970. "Ethnographic Salvage and the Shaping of Anthropology." *American Anthropologist*, n.s., 72 (6): 1289–99.

Harry, Debra. 2005. "Acts of Self-Determination and Self-Defense: Indigenous Peoples' Responses to Biocolonialism." In *Rights and Liberties in the Biotech Age: Why We Need a Genetic Bill of Rights*, ed. Sheldon Krimsky and Peter Shorett, 87–98. Lanham MD: Roman and Littlefield.

Hinton, Leanne. 1994. *Flutes of Fire: Essays on California Indian Languages*. Berkeley: Heyday.

Hogeland, Frank L., and Kim Hogeland. 2007. *First Families: A Photographic History of California Indians*. Berkeley: Heyday Books.

Hurtado, Albert L. 1988. *Indian Survival on the California Frontier*. New Haven: Yale University Press.

Hymes, Dell H. 1996. *Ethnography, Linguistics, Narrative Inequality: Toward an Understanding of Voice*. Bristol PA: Taylor & Francis.

———. 2004. *"In Vain I Tried to Tell You": Essays in Native American Poetics*. Lincoln: University of Nebraska Press.

Kaplan, Sarah. 2015. "Denali or McKinley? How a 19th-Century Political 'Joke' Turned into a 119-Year-Long Debate." *Washington Post*, August 31.

Kroeber, Alfred L. 1925. *Handbook of the Indians of California*. Bulletin 78 of the Bureau of American Ethnology, Smithsonian Institution. Washington DC: Government Printing Office.

Kroeber, Theodora. 2011 [1961]. *Ishi in Two Worlds: A Biography of the Last Wild Indian in North America*. Berkeley: University of California Press.

Kroskrity, Paul, and Margaret Field. 2011. *Native American Language Ideologies: Beliefs, Practices, and Struggles in Indian Country*. Tucson: University of Arizona Press.

Kroskrity, Paul, and Barbara Meek. 2017. *Engaging Indigenous Publics: Linguistic Anthropology in a Collaborative Key*. Abingdon-on-Thames: Routledge.

Lindsay, Brendan C. 2012. *Murder State: California's Native American Genocide, 1846–1873*. Lincoln: University of Nebraska Press.

Lomawaima, Tsianina K., and Teresa L. McCarty. 2006. *To Remain an Indian: Lessons in Democracy from a Century of Native American Education*. New York: Teachers College Press.

Lowie, Robert. 1915. "Oral Tradition and History." *American Anthropologist*, n.s., 17 (3): 597–99.

Lowry, Leonard. 1999. Interviewed in 1993 by Helen Blue. Edited by Cathleen Coles, University of Nevada Oral History Program. http://contentdm.library.unr.edu/cdm /compoundobject/collection/unohp/id/2503/rec/15.

Luthin, Herbert W. 2002. *Surviving through the Days: Translations of Native California Stories and Songs*. Berkeley: University of California Press.

MacLoon, John, ed. 2008. *Muscular Christianity in the Colonial and Post-Colonial World*. New York: Routledge.

Madley, Benjamin. 2016. *An American Genocide: The United States and the California Indian Catastrophe*. New Haven: Yale University Press.

Margolin, Malcolm, ed. 1993. *The Way We Lived: California Indian Stories, Songs, and Reminiscences*. Berkeley: Heyday.

McCarty, Teresa. 2013. *Language Planning and Policy in Native America: History, Theory, Praxis*. Tonowanda NY: Multilingual Matters.

Meek, Barbra A. 2010 *We Are Our Language: An Ethnography of Language Revitalization in a Northern Athabascan Community*. Tucson: University of Arizona Press.

Merlan, Francesca. 2009. "Indigeneity: Local and Global." *Current Anthropology* 50 (3): 303–33.

Middleton, Beth Rose. 2001. "'We Were Here, We Are Here, We Will Always Be Here': A Political Ecology of Healing in Mountain Maidu Country." PhD diss., University of California, Berkeley.

———. 2011. *Trust in the Land: New Directions in Tribal Conservation*. Tucson: University of Arizona Press.

———. 2014. "ChuChuYamBa / Soda Rock: Toward an Applied Critical Geographic Perspective on Traditional Cultural Properties (TCPS)." *Human Geography* 7 (2).

———. 2015 "Jahát Jatítotòdom*: Toward an Indigenous Political Ecology." In *International Handbook of Political Ecology*, ed. Raymond L. Bryant, 561–76. Northhampton MA: Edward Elgar.

Miller, Mabel L. 1896. "The So-Called California 'Diggers.'" *Appleton's Popular Science Monthly* 50 (December): 201–14.

Nevins, M. Eleanor, with Thomas Nevins, Paul Ethelbah, and Genevieve Ethelbah. 2004. "'He Became an Eagle': A Contemporary Western Apache Oral Narrative." In *Voices from the Four Directions: Contemporary Translations of Native American Oral Literature*, ed. Brian Swann, 283–302. Lincoln: University of Nebraska Press.

———, with Thomas J. Nevins. 2012. "'They Do Not Know How to Ask': Pedagogy,

Storytelling, and the Ironies of Language Endangerment on the Fort Apache Reservation." In *Telling Stories in the Face of Danger*, ed. Paul Kroskrity. Norman: University of Oklahoma Press.

———, with Paul Ethelbah and Genevieve Ethelbah. 2013a. "Ndah Ch'ii'n Western Apache Journey between Worlds." In *Inside Dazzling Mountains: Native Literatures of the American Southwest*, ed. David Kotak. Lincoln: University of Nebraska Press.

———. 2013b. *Lessons from Fort Apache: Beyond Language Endangerment and Maintenance*. Blackwell Studies in Discourse and Culture series. Hoboken NJ: Wiley-Blackwell.

O'Neill, Sean. 2008. *Cultural Contact and Linguistic Relativity among the Indians of Northwestern California*. Norman: University of Oklahoma Press.

Perley, Bernard. 2001. *Defying Maliseet Language Death: Emergent Vitalities of Language, Culture, and Identity in Eastern Canada*. Lincoln: University of Nebraska Press.

Powers, Stephen. 1877. *Tribes of California*. Department of the Interior, U.S. Geographic and Geological Survey of the Rocky Mountain Region. Contributions to North American Ethnology, vol. 3. Washington DC: Government Printing Office.

Reyner, Jon, and Jeanne Eder. 2006. *American Indian Education: A History*. Norman: University of Oklahoma Press.

Riddell, Francis A. 1978. "Maidu and Konkow." In *Handbook of North American Indians*, vol. 8, *California*, ed. Robert F. Heizer, 370–86. Washington DC: Smithsonian Institution.

Sarris, Greg. 1993. *Keeping Slug Woman Alive: A Holistic Approach to American Indian Texts*. Berkeley: University of California Press.

———. 1994. *The Sound of Rattles and Clappers: A Collection of New California Indian Writing*. Sun Tracks series. Tucson: University of Arizona Press.

———. 2013. *Mabel McKay: Weaving the Dream*. Berkeley: University of California Press.

Seymour, Susan. 2015. *Cora Du Bois: Anthropologist, Diplomat, Agent*. Lincoln: University of Nebraska Press.

Shipley, William F. 1963. *Maidu Texts and Dictionary*. University of California Publications in Linguistics, vol. 33. Berkeley: University of California Press.

———. 1964. *Maidu Grammar*. University of California Publications in Linguistics, vol. 41. Berkeley: University of California Press.

———. 1986. "Maidu Literary Style." In *In Honor of Mary Haas: From the Haas Festival Conference on Native American Linguistics*, ed. William Shipley, 705–14. New York: Mouton de Gruyter.

———. 1991. *The Maidu Indian Myths and Stories of Hanc'ibyjim*. Foreword by Gary Snyder. Berkeley CA: Heyday Books.

Shipley, William (translator), and Daniel O. Stolpe (illustrator). 2002. *The Creation as the Maidu Told It = púktim*. Santa Cruz: Native Images Editions.

———. 2003. *The Adversaries = hómpajtotokyc'om*. Santa Cruz: Native Images Editions.

———. 2004. *Love and Death = hybý'ym masý wónom*. Santa Cruz: Native Images
   Editions.
———. 2005. *Coyote the Spoiler = wépam wasátykim*. Santa Cruz: Native Images
   Editions.
Smith, Linda Tuhiwai. 1999. *Decolonizing Methodologies: Research and Indigenous
   Peoples*. London: Zed.
Smith, Stacey L. 2014. *Freedom's Frontier: California and the Struggle over Unfree
   Labor, Emancipation, and Reconstruction*. Chapel Hill: University of North
   Carolina Press.
Spack, Ruth. 2002. *America's Second Tongue: American Indian Education and the
   Ownership of English, 1860–1900*. Lincoln: University of Nebraska Press.
Spagna, Ana Maria. 2015. "A Displaced Tribe Reclaims Sacred Land: The Mountain
   Maidu Return to Their Valley but the Work of Reclamation Never Ends." *High
   Country News*, September 14, 2015.
Swanton, John R. 1902. Review of *Maidu Myths* by Roland B. Dixon. *American
   Anthropologist*, n.s., 4 (3): 524–26.
Swanton, John R., and Roland Dixon. 1914. "Primitive American History." *American
   Anthropologist* 16 (3): 376–412.
Tedlock, Dennis, and Bruce Mannheim, eds. 1995. *The Dialogic Emergence of Culture*.
   Urbana: University of Illinois Press.
Thomas, David H. 2000. *Skull Wars: Kennewick Man, Archaeology, and the Battle for
   Native American Identity*. New York: Basic Books.
Tozzer, A. M., and A. L. Kroeber. 1945. "Roland Burridge Dixon." *American
   Anthropologist* 47: 104–18.
Valborg, Helen, and Farrell Cunningham. 2007. "The Mountain Maidu Homeland:
   Native and Anthropological Interpretations of Cultural Identity." In *Great Basin
   Rock Art: Archaeological Perspectives*, ed. Angus R. Quinlan, 20–33. Reno:
   University of Nevada Press.
Vizenor, Gerald, ed. 1997. *Native American Literature: A Brief Introduction and
   Anthology*. Longman Literary Mosaic series. Harlow: Longman.
Weaver, Jace, Craig S. Womack, and Robert Warrior. 2006. *American Indian Literary
   Nationalism*. Albuquerque: University of New Mexico Press.
White, Richard. 1998. "The Gold Rush: Consequences and Contingencies." *California
   History* 77 (1): 42–55.
———. 2003. "Information, Markets, and Corruption: Transcontinental Railroads in
   the Gilded Age." *Journal of American History* 90 (1): 19–43.
———. 2011. *Railroaded: The Transcontinentals and the Making of Modern America*.
   New York: Norton.
Zinn, Howard. 2003. *A People's History of United States: 1942 to Present*. New York:
   HarperCollins.

INDEX

Page numbers in italics refer to illustrations

www.ingramcontent.com/pod-product-compliance
Lightning Source LLC
Chambersburg PA
CBHW081147020726
47504CB00009B/2027